THE MAN
JESUS

Fact and Legend

Acknowledgement is given to Michael Noakes
for the use of his artwork (the portrait of
Michael McCrum).

THE MAN JESUS

Fact and Legend

Michael McCrum

JANUS PUBLISHING COMPANY
London, England

First published in Great Britain 1999
by Janus Publishing Company Limited,
76 Great Titchfield Street,
London W1P 7AF

www.januspublishing.co.uk

A CIP catalogue record for this book
is available from the British Library.

ISBN 1 85756 452 9

Phototypeset in 12 on 14 Palatino
by Keyboard Services, Luton, Beds

Cover design Peter Clarke

Printed and bound in Great Britain

To Robert, Elizabeth, Mark and Stephen
and their families

Contents

Preface

Most people have some idea who Jesus was: that he was a holy man living many centuries ago in Palestine. But that is the extent of their knowledge.

Many use the names Jesus and Christ as swear words, without meaning any disrespect to, or any connexion with, the holy man of Palestine. Others think that they know quite a lot about Jesus and do not like what they know – his references to hellfire at the day of judgement, for instance. His demands on them seem out of date, excessive, or misguided. Some think that he never existed at all or that, if he did, his importance has been greatly exaggerated.

These critics are not willing to consider the evidence but instinctively prefer to write it off. They claim, with some justification, that Jesus was not born in AD 1 in a manger in Bethlehem, nor was his mother a virgin; that Mary was engaged to Joseph but had not yet married him; that Jesus was not descended from King David; that there was no special star to guide anyone to Jesus's birthplace, nor was he visited by three wise men or kings, or even shepherds; that Jesus and his parents did not travel to Egypt to avoid possible assassination by King Herod's soldiers; that while Jesus was no doubt a remarkable teacher, healer and prophetic figure, he was not divine; that he was devout, worshipful, and charismatic, but not *the* Son of God.

Many of those who believe in him as in some sense divine, God but also human, have a severely limited understanding of what modern scholars now think about him and his message.

There is a considerable gap between the critical historical approach to the study of the New Testament with its portrayal of Jesus on the one hand, and on the other what is usually conveyed about him as the faith of the Bible in church worship and sermons. During the last three decades in particular the quest for the historical Jesus has been pursued by many scholars with renewed determination and great energy, but comparatively little of their discussions and conclusions has reached the man or woman in the pew, or the interested but agnostic or atheistic inquirer. When they have reached a wider public they have sometimes shocked those holding traditional beliefs.

My aim here is to set out as clearly, directly, and succinctly as possible what we now think we may with some confidence say about the man Jesus as a historical person. Since Christians always claim that their religion is founded on historical fact, this is clearly important. My approach, however, is minimalist, to try to set out what modern scholars accept as historical fact, rather than their often elaborate and hypothetical theories about Jesus's significance, a plain man's view of what can and cannot be said about the events in Jesus's life recorded in the New Testament. I write as a layman who, though not a specialist theologian, has for many years studied the historical writings of the first century AD and who has been surprised that so few ordained ministers have tried to explain to their congregations this gap between the two portraits of Jesus.

It will not, however, be in any sense a biography because the sources of our information about him give us little biographical detail. The four evangelists did not set out to write history, but to effect belief in Jesus as Messiah, Son of God, and Son of Man. Apart from the stories of his birth, most of which cannot be regarded as historical, and one story in Luke about a visit to Jerusalem at the age of twelve, we know nothing about Jesus until his baptism by John when he was in his thirties. Even then we are given none of the background that we would find in a biography – his appearance, his physique and health, his upbringing and education, his training for work, his job (except for a passing reference to his being a carpenter or the son of a carpenter), the length of his ministry, or his age at his death. Indeed, apart from his six weeks in the wilderness, the events recorded in Mark's gospel could all have occurred within four weeks.

The great bulk of what we know relates to the last three or so years of his life, his so-called ministry, before he was crucified, and much of that is controversial because of the nature and purpose of our main sources, the gospels.

In this brief history I have tried to answer an important aspect of Professor Hodgson's famous question: 'What must the truth be, and have been, if it appeared like that to men who thought and wrote as they did?' To this end I shall first consider the non-Christian sources and the nature and date of the Christian sources, then the historicity of the birth stories, followed by an account of his ministry and teaching, an assessment of his 'miracles', and an explanation of why he was crucified, with a discussion of when it took place.

Finally I shall touch on the trans-historical event of the resurrection, for the history of Jesus would be of small significance if his life had ended with his death.

The Right Reverend Peter Walker, former Bishop of Ely, and my second son, Mark, kindly read my typescript and made most useful suggestions for improvement, and my wife, eldest son Robert, and Professor John Roach also gave me encouragement. To all these I am most grateful.

Synopsis

Historical sources   The authors of the gospels were not aiming to write history as we understand it. Their purpose was to proclaim Jesus as Messiah (everyone's saviour), Son of God.

Four non-Christian historians, contemporary with the early church, independently confirm that Jesus lived and died in the first century AD.

The earliest Christian historical evidence is provided by Paul's Letters, written within twenty years of the crucifixion. The four gospels, which do not pretend to be biographies, developed independently of each other later out of the strong oral tradition of the early Christian communities.

Historical background   The importance of the Jewish and Hellenistic background cannot be exaggerated. Roman rule, mediated by client-kings, barely impinged. The Jews believed that they were a special people, worshipping one God whose presence was worshipped in the Temple at Jerusalem.

Birth The birth stories are not historical, but were composed (mainly out of Old Testament material) to show that he who had by his death and resurrection been revealed as Messiah had a special status from birth. Jesus was not born in Bethlehem, nor were there three wise men, a star, shepherds, or a flight to Egypt to escape from Herod.

Jesus was born in 5/4 BC, not AD 1, a date which was due to a monkish calendar-maker's miscalculation.

Baptism Jesus was baptised by John the Baptist, but the supernatural additions to the story are not historical.

Jesus's Ministry probably lasted three and a half years, AD 29–33.

Titles The three titles (Son of Man, Son of God, Messiah) are all used in different ways at different times by the evangelists, so it is not clear precisely how Jesus regarded his relationship to God. But he undoubtedly believed that he had a special status with God.

Miracles The healing miracles are most likely to have been true. Jesus had remarkable healing gifts, the public practice of which helped to create a group of disciples. The other miracles are best explained as representing the beliefs of the early Christians, in Jesus's compassion, for instance.

Parables Jesus was a great teacher who used vivid stories to describe the kingdom of God which was the central theme of his teaching. But several parables have disputed meanings.

Kingdom of God Jesus's view of the kingdom was not political; he saw it as an ideal community where God's chosen people would be restored to a full relationship with God.

Conflict Though Jesus's mission was to all Israel, he created controversy because his teaching went beyond Jews' current thinking, in particular claiming that Moses's law did not go far enough.

Conflict with his family arose from his belief in the urgent priority of establishing the kingdom.

Supporters Jesus had the support of fourteen apostles (called the Twelve after the Twelve Tribes of Israel), several devoted women, possibly seventy-two disciples sent on a special mission, and a few secret sympathizers.

Transfiguration This was probably a post-Resurrection experience placed before it by later tradition in the early church.

Crucifixion Historical evidence strongly confirms that Jesus was crucified on 3 April AD 33, condemned to death on the one hand by the Jews for supposed blasphemy but in reality rabble-rousing thought by the chief priests to be dangerously subversive, and on the other by Pontius Pilate, who alone could order executions, at the Jews' request on the bogus charge of claiming to be King of the Jews who could thus be seen as a threat to Roman rule.

That Jesus was crucified by Roman soldiers is the best-attested event in the New Testament, but much of the passion narrative has Old Testament resonances which suggest that some of the attendant circumstances are not entirely historical. The placard on the cross and the presence of women are, however, probably genuine.

Resurrection   A trans-historical event. Despite many discrepancies between the gospel accounts the main aspects are clear: the empty tomb, the women's visit, Peter's reaction to the news, the apostles' overwhelming conviction that somehow Jesus had risen from the dead and was alive. On their consequent confidence, in marked contrast to their demoralized despair at the crucifixion, the Christian church was founded and has flourished ever since.

Ascension   The account is found only in the writings of Luke who gives two different versions, so it is historically doubtful. However, it can be taken as representing the final movement of Jesus from this world.

1

The non-Christian Sources

Three Romans writing in the first quarter of the second century AD provide independent, if indirect, evidence of Jesus's existence. Their references are, not surprisingly, brief, for Jesus was at this time only a minor figure on the world stage. Two of these authors were historians; Tacitus (c. AD 55–117) and Suetonius (c. AD 70–?130). Tacitus in his *Annals*, some eighteen books covering the reigns of the emperors Tiberius, Gaius, Claudius, and Nero (AD 14–68), gives the fullest and most detailed account. In discussing the great fire of Rome in AD 64 he mentions that Nero, in order to divert rumours that he had instigated it, laid the blame on the Christians and had them cruelly and publicly punished.

'Their founder, Christ,' he wrote, 'had been executed in the reign of Tiberius (AD 14–37) by Pontius Pilate, governor of Judaea. But despite this temporary setback the pernicious superstition had broken out anew, not only in Judaea (where the trouble had started) but even in Rome where all things horrible or shameful in the world collect and find a vogue. First, Nero had Christians who confessed their faith arrested. Then on their information large numbers of others were condemned – not so much for incendiarism as because they were hated by the human race... They were torn to pieces by dogs, or crucified, or made into torches to be lit after dark as substitutes for daylight... Despite their guilt as Christians, and the ruthless punishment it deserved, the victims were pitied. For it was thought that they were being sacrificed to one man's brutality rather than to the national interest.'[1]

Suetonius, who is also concerned to mention the Christians because they were troublemakers, refers to them twice, though more briefly. In his biography of the emperor Claudius, who ruled from AD 41–54, he reports the expulsion from Rome of 'the Jews who under the influence of Chrestus (*sic*) were constantly causing disturbances.'[2] This expulsion occurred in AD 49, only sixteen years after Jesus's death. In so short a time had the Christian gospel spread to the capital of the Roman Empire and created antagonism in the Jewish community there. His second reference[3] is to the same incidents as those reported by Tacitus: under Nero (AD 54–68) 'punishment was inflicted on the Christians, a class of men given to a new and mischievous superstition.'

The third Roman, Pliny the younger (*c.* AD 61–*c.* 112), a friend of Tacitus, who about AD 110 was appointed governor of the province of Bithynia-Pontus (in NW Asia Minor) by the emperor Trajan, in a long letter to his master asking how to handle the trials of Christians (Is the mere profession of Christianity a crime?), describes Christian worship as follows:

2

'They claimed that their only fault or mistake was their custom of meeting regularly before daybreak to sing a hymn in alternate verses to Christ as if to a God and to promise with an oath ... not to commit theft, fraud or adultery, break their word, or deny a trust when summoned to hand it over.'[4]

Trajan's tolerant reply enabled Pliny to avoid persecuting Christians.[5]

The only other significant non-Christian early reference to Jesus is to be found in the *Antiquities* of the Jewish historian Josephus. Born in AD 37/8, a priest of aristocratic origin and Pharisaic education, he became pro-Roman and after the fall of Jerusalem in AD 70 settled in Rome and became a Roman citizen. Author of seven books on the Jewish war against Rome, published between AD 75 and 79, twenty books on Jewish antiquities including his autobiography in an appendix, published in 93/4, and an apologia for Judaism in two books, he provides the most important evidence on first-century Jewish history.

In *Antiquities*[6] he refers briefly to the martyrdom of James in AD 62, 'the brother of Jesus called the Messiah', and writes more fully about Jesus:

'About this time there lived Jesus, a wise man, [if indeed one ought to call him a man]. For he was one who wrought surprising feats and was a teacher of such people as accept the truth gladly. He won over many Jews and many of the Greeks. [He was the Messiah.] When Pilate, upon hearing him accused by men of the highest standing amongst us, had condemned him to be crucified, those who had in the first place come to love him did not give up their affection for him. [On the third day he appeared to them restored to life, for the prophets of God had prophesied these and countless other marvellous things about him.] And the tribe of Christians, so called after him, has still to this day not disappeared.' (*Translated by L. H. Feldman*)[7]

While it is likely that this passage was doctored by Christian scribes who transmitted it, most modern scholars accept that, with the bracketed sentences omitted, the paragraph is probably an accurate summary of what an educated Jew living at the turn of the century would have known about Jesus and his followers.

Other possible Jewish references, for instance in the Talmud, are of uncertain interpretation.

The non-Christian sources are mainly important in confirming that in the first century AD no one doubted Jesus's historical existence. They also provide independent confirmation of some aspects of the earliest Christian tradition about Jesus, such as that Jesus had a brother called James, that he was a teacher who had devoted followers, that he performed miracles, and that his death was violent.

NOTES
1. Tacitus, *Annals* xv. 44: 3–4.
2. Suetonius, *Claudius* 25: 4; Acts 18: 2.
3. Suetonius, *Nero* 16:2.
4. Pliny, *Epist.* X. xcvi.
5. Pliny, *op. cit.* X. xcvii.
6. Josephus, *Antiq.* xx: 200.
7. Josephus, *op. cit.* xviii: 63–4.

2

The Christian sources

A brief chronology of the seventy years after the crucifixion (3 April, AD 33, or possibly 7 April, AD 30) gives the background to the Christian witness.

36	Stephen martyred; Saul converted.
38	Paul's first visit to Jerusalem (Galatians 1: 18).
Prob. 47–8	Paul's first missionary journey (Acts 13: 1–14.28).
49	Paul meets the Apostolic Council in Jerusalem (Acts 15: 1–29; Gal. 2: 1–10).
Early Fifties	Paul's Letters to the Thessalonians I and possibly II.
50–54	Paul's second missionary journey (he meets Gallio in Corinth in 51/2, Acts 18: 12–17).
51	Paul's Letter to the Galatians.
51–53	Paul's Letters to the Corinthians I and II.

53–54	Paul's Letter to the Romans
c.55–58	Paul's third missionary journey (Acts 18: 23–21: 17).
58–60	Paul in prison in Caesarea. Paul's Letter to the Philippians.
Prob. 60	Paul is taken to Rome.
c.60–61	Paul's Letters to Philemon and the Colossians.
c.61–62	Paul in Rome.
c.65	Paul probably killed (at the same time as Peter) after great fire in July 64 (or possibly in 62 at the end of two years of custody).
65–70	Mark's gospel, written for a persecuted Christian community living outside Palestine, probably in Rome.
Before 70	Letter to the Hebrews (author unknown).
80–85	Matthew's gospel, for a Christian community in Syria, possibly at Antioch.
80–85	Luke's gospel and Acts may have been written earlier towards the end of the reign of the emperor Vespasian (AD 69–79). He wrote for a gentile Christian community in a Greek-speaking area.
85–90 (at earliest)	John's gospel, for the Christian community at Ephesus.

These dates, approximate though most of them are, show clearly that references to Jesus's life and death in Paul's letters and letters attributed to Paul, albeit few, are important evidence. Not only did Paul meet Peter within five or six years of Jesus's crucifixion, but most of his letters preceded and all were independent of the gospels' much fuller accounts. Though written before the gospels, they were published after them. So just as Paul did not know the gospels, the evangelists did not know Paul's letters.

In two of Paul's letters which are certainly his composition we are told of Jesus's fundamentally divine nature (Phil. 2: 6), that at the same time he is fully human, and that he was declared Son of God by his resurrection from the dead (Rom. 1: 3–4). It is of striking significance that Paul was preaching the same message as the gospels some years before they were themselves composed – good evidence of how early was the Christian tradition. His account (in 1 Cor. 11: 23–26) of the Last Supper also provides the earliest confirmation of the same meal as that described in the gospels. In the letter to the Hebrews, of unknown authorship but possibly written by Barnabas or Apollos, we are told that Jesus shared our flesh and blood so that through death he might break its power and free us from fear of it (Heb. 2: 14–15). In a later passage (4: 15–5.8) the same author asserts that Jesus Christ, Son of God, was tested in every way as are we and that God delivered him from the grave. This profoundly theological letter, emphasising the supremacy of Christ, was written before all the gospels except possibly Mark.

Two other New Testament authors, apart from the four gospel writers, who seem to provide independent confirmation of a few of the details of Jesus's life (2 Pet. 1: 16–18 on the Transfiguration and 1 John 1: 1–3), were probably writing in the last quarter of the first century. Our key sources, however, on the details of Jesus's life and teaching are the four gospels. But it is essential to realize that they are not literally true in all respects. There are many instances of disagreement on substance and detail which confirm this judgment. To take only three, even the most cursory glance at the two family trees (the genealogies) of Jesus given by Matthew and Luke at the start of their gospels reveal major discrepancies (Matt. 1: 1–17, Luke 3: 23–38); secondly, Matthew's version of the Lord's Prayer differs from Luke's (6: 9–15, Luke 11: 2–4); thirdly, the words spoken by Jesus at the Last Supper are different in Luke (22. 20) and in Paul's first letter to the Corinthians (I Cor. 11: 25) from those in Matthew and Mark. In the former he says, 'This is the new covenant in my blood.' In the latter he says, 'This is my blood.' These and other discrepancies may be due to the problems inherent in translating Jesus's words (in Aramaic) into the Greek of the gospels, an altogether unrelated language.

Not only do the gospels sometimes differ in their descriptions of the same events, but the first three gospels (Matthew, Mark, and Luke), commonly called the synoptic gospels because they are so much like each other when looked at side by side, are quite different from John in style and content. (Synoptic is a Greek word meaning 'seen together'.)

For instance, in John there are no birth stories, and Jesus's ministry lasts more than two years rather than less than one. John sets Jesus's cleansing of the Temple in Jerusalem at the start of Jesus's ministry, the synoptics at the end. In John, Jerusalem is indeed much more the scene of Jesus's activity than Galilee. The procedure at

Jesus's trial is informal in John, formal in the other three gospels.

As to Jesus's teaching, there are few parables in John, and the kingdom of God, a constant theme in the synoptic gospels, is mentioned only once in John. In John we find long theological discourses by Jesus about himself and his relationship to God and his disciples, whereas the synoptic authors set out his teaching in short pithy stories and sayings such as the Sermon on the Mount. John uses the word 'sign' for Jesus's miracles and omits all mention of exorcisms. John's gospel, although composed much later than the three synoptics, was almost certainly written without any direct use of them.

Although there is not a complete consensus about the relationship of the three synoptic gospels to each other, most scholars now accept that Mark was the first gospel, of whose 666 verses Matthew made use of over 600 and Luke of 350, both independently of each other. A further 230 verses (consisting mostly of Jesus's sayings, probably recorded in writing) are common to both Matthew and Luke, and these are called Q material (Quelle is the German word for source). Verses peculiar to Matthew amount to only 230, and to Luke something over 400. A diagram based on that of B. H. Streeter,[1] but modified, may help to make the relationship clear:

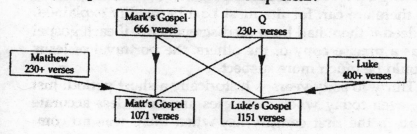

9

What can be said of all the gospels is that, though to some extent appearing to be biographical and not unlike some ancient classical biographies, they are not biographies in our sense but essentially accounts of the passion and resurrection with a semi-biographical preface. They are primarily treatises designed to convince the reader that Jesus is divine, the Son of God, and the Saviour of mankind. To that end they combine all that tradition has handed down with what can be attributed to Jewish scripture (our Old Testament) as probable prophecy. Although named after historical persons, the gospels were not written by eyewitnesses of the events of Jesus's life and death, but by anonymous authors writing some thirty to sixty years later who were translating, into Greek, sayings and experiences originally expressed in a Semitic language. During those years there will have been several stages in the development of the stories and teaching, oral at the start, then written; this is how tradition is formed. Probably as early as the Thirties, the passion story would have been developed, and by the mid Forties most of the account found in the synoptic gospels would have taken shape, possibly even in written form. At each stage in each community there would have been a strong determination to convey as accurate, honest, and convincing a portrait of Jesus as possible. Such discrepancies as there are can for the most part be readily explained. Indeed if there had been no discrepancies, if each gospel was a precise copy of the others, the portrayal of Jesus would be much more suspect.

Thirty to sixty years is historically a short period. Just as, even today when memories are much less accurate than in the first century AD, when there was no competition from the printed word, there are still people alive who remember the First World War (now more than eighty years ago) and can recount their experiences of it, and many more who have clear recollections of the Second World War of sixty years ago, so we have good reason to believe that the gospel story is in its main outline founded in fact. Paul's account, in the First Letter to the Christians in Corinth (I Cor. 15: 5–6), of Jesus's post-resurrection appearances to over five hundred people, most of whom were still alive when he wrote in the early Fifties, is undoubted confirmation of the tradition which was later accepted and written down by the authors of the four gospels. Moreover, since there was widespread use of wax-coated writing tablets during Jesus's lifetime, it is conceivable that some of the first disciples might have made written notes of his teachings and sayings.

Scholars who try to make out that we can know very little of Jesus's life and who emphasise the discrepancies in the New Testament, fail to understand how determined the early Christians must have been not to give a false picture of one who had come to be their venerated hero. Such errors as there clearly are (for example, Luke's misdating of the census under Quirinius, Legate of Syria) are due to human frailty, not carelessness, dishonesty, or fraud.

Although we do not possess the original texts of the four gospels, but only copies of copies, their reliability has long been confirmed by a careful study of the earliest manuscripts that have survived. While the first copy of the whole New Testament cannot be dated earlier than the fourth century AD, much earlier portions go back as far as the second century AD (e.g. John 18 in the Bodmer

11

papyrus). Moreover no non-Christian manuscript can be dated as early as the Christian. There is, for instance, no earlier manuscript of Tacitus than the eighth century AD. Since the more often a manuscript is copied the greater likelihood there is of mistakes creeping in, the very early date of the gospels provides significant testimony to their accuracy.

By using a few well tried methods of interpretation we can sometimes discern which elements in the gospels are likely to be strictly historical and which not. How the evangelists dealt with traditions that they had received can often be assessed. This is most readily apparent in noting how Matthew and Luke modify Mark. It is often possible to differentiate between one of Jesus's original teachings, statements, or actions and its modification by an evangelist to fit a later context. For example, Jesus's words recorded in Matt. 18: 20 ('Where two or three are gathered in my name, there am I in the midst of them') are not appropriate to their setting in chapter 18 of Matthew, but are wholly appropriate to post-Easter practice when disciples would meet together for worship.

Three further methods are also used to assess historicity: first, a tradition is probably authentic if it seems likely to have embarrassed the early church; for instance, Mark's reference (3: 21) to Jesus being thought out of his mind by his opponents is omitted by Matthew and Luke. Second, if a traditional account of a saying or action by Jesus is dissimilar to early Jewish custom as well as to the practice of the early Christians, it is likely to be historical; for example, Jesus's attitude to fasting, which offended the Pharisees *and* was questioned by the disciples of John the Baptist (Mark 2: 18–22). Third, if one

of Jesus's sayings or actions has two or more references in different contexts, it is probably authentic; for
example, Jesus's friendly attitude to tax collectors which
incurred strong criticism (Mark 2: 15; Luke 19: 7). But we
need to keep in mind at all times when reading the
gospels in a modern translation how very different social
customs and expectations were then and how different
the language in which they were expressed.

The particular names that we attach to the authors of
the four gospels were moreover not attached until the
second century. When first composed, the gospels'
authors were, as I said earlier, anonymous. For anonymity
was then regarded as giving greater authority. Irenaeus,
Bishop of Lyons,[2] was the first Christian to name all four.
Writing in about 180, he reveals his knowledge of the
gospels as we know them and wrote about the one gospel
in fourfold form. Until at least the early years of the
second century, Christians were uninterested in who
wrote which gospel. From the extant writings of the early
fathers such as Irenaeus we can advance a plausible
theory, but no more than this, that when Christians
became interested in gospel authorship they sought
names that fitted best each particular gospel.

The first gospel was called after Matthew possibly
because only this gospel (9: 9) calls the tax-collector who
became Jesus's disciple Matthew. Mark (2: 14) and Luke
(5: 27) refer to a tax-collector called Levi as one of Jesus's
disciples and associate his name with the scene at the tax
office where Matthew worked and from where he was
called to discipleship. Was it not reasonable that Matthew
the tax-collector knew his own name and wished it to be
remembered in that remarkable context? Moreover, there

was a tradition that Matthew collected sayings, and these are prominent in the first gospel. The author of this gospel, whose command of Greek, knowledge of the Old Testament, and theological outlook are plainly superior to a tax-collector's, would probably have been a member of a church such as Antioch in Syria founded by the apostle.

Mark's gospel, with its plain prose style and intimate knowledge of Palestine, was assigned to him because of his relationship to Peter (I Pet. 5: 13; Acts 12: 12), to whom the early Christians would have assigned it if it was not generally known that Peter did not himself write a gospel.

Luke's name was probably chosen for the third gospel because it appears to have been written by the author of Acts, and Acts contains passages where 'we' is used rather than 'they', which seems to indicate that Luke 'the beloved physician' of Paul's letters and fellow-worker (Col. 4: 14; 2 Tim. 4: 11) was present as recorder or diarist.

John's name was given to the fourth gospel because he was traditionally regarded as 'the disciple whom Jesus loved', who, though referred to as present at that memorable farewell picnic on the beach beside the Sea of Tiberias (John 21: 1–23), is specifically not named, whereas other disciples are, such as Peter and Thomas who were also there. He was closely associated with the Christian community in Ephesus.

The gospels, our main, indeed best, source of information about Jesus, are deceptively simple on a superficial reading. But the more we study them, the more complex, significant, and profound they prove to be. Despite their discrepancies and occasional conflict of testimony they are fundamentally reliable documents which have survived the most searching examination by generations of scholars and continue to have a remarkable relevance to our modern world.

NOTES
1. B. H. Streeter, *The Four Gospels* (London 1936), p. 150.
2. Irenaeus, *Against Heresies* (Edinburgh 1868), III. 1; III. 11.

3

Ancient historians

All historians are the creatures of their times; what we
expect of historians today is very different from what
those living in the first century AD expected from the
historians of their age. Today we look primarily for
accuracy and objectivity; only secondarily for lively,
imaginative writing, a good story. Then, partly at least
because history was close to other literary genres such as
poetry and tragedy, fact and fiction were intertwined to
make what the author thought would give the best effect,
would please most. Cicero's claim,[1] written in the first
century BC, that truth is the standard by which all history
is judged, while in poetry the standard is usually
pleasure, was only partially borne out in the practice of
Roman historians such as Tacitus and Suetonius, who
wrote soon after the New Testament authors.

The use that such historians made of the documents
that they had was inadequate and often surprising. They
made little use of written sources, and when they did,
they did not check the information, often mistranslating

or misinterpreting it. They accepted oral tradition when it was untrustworthy, even when it was plainly fictitious. Sometimes they excused themselves by describing their information as rumours, but gave these rumours currency nevertheless. The digressions, often quite long ones, which they inserted from time to time, are the equivalent of our footnotes, and the speeches which they put into the mouths of their characters were usually inauthentic and designed to offer a lively explanation of the background to events.

In his first book[2] the fifth-century BC Greek historian, Thucydides, described his method. The famous speech by the Athenian statesman Pericles, for instance, written long after it was supposed to have been made, was never made by Pericles, but was Thucydides' idealised account of Athenian democracy. Where we can compare the text of a speech with a historian's version, we find only a slight resemblance. A speech by the emperor Claudius[3] (AD 41–54) to the Roman senate, which has been preserved in bronze at Lyons, bears only a marginal similarity to the version found in the Roman historian Tacitus.[4]

It is, then, reasonable to suppose that speeches or sayings attributed to Jesus in the gospels were not precisely as he spoke them. Such a view is confirmed by the differences that we find between gospel accounts of the same event, as for instance in the Beatitudes. Did Jesus say that 'the poor in spirit' or 'the poor' were blessed? 'The hungry' or 'those that hunger and thirst for righteousness'? A comparison of Matthew 5: 3–12 and Luke 6: 20–23 shows many other dissimilarities. There is, for example, no mention in Luke of the merciful, or the pure in heart, or the peacemakers being blessed.

The New Testament writers, however, differed in their main aim from other ancient historians. They doubtless made similar errors through ignorance and lack of appropriate information, or through personal prejudice; Luke, for example, places the birth of Jesus during the reign of Herod the Great (who died in 4 BC) but also dates it to the time of Quirinius's census AD 6 (1: 5; 2: 2). As we saw earlier, their purpose, however, was not primarily literary. Everything that they wrote, the stories about Jesus and his sayings, though not always actual events, was genuinely characteristic of him or designed to show who he really was. They had such faith in the revelation of Jesus as the Christ that they felt bound to use all their imaginative powers to convince their readers of its reality. The picture that they thus created was fundamentally truer than a plain biographical account would have been.

NOTES
1. Cicero, Laws I. i.5; Michael Grant, *Greek and Roman Historians*, p. 30.
2. Thucydides, *History of the Peloponnesian War*, I. 22.1; Michael Grant, *op. cit.*, p. 47.
3. E. M. Smallwood, *Documents Illustrating the Principates of Gaius, Claudius, and Nero* (Cambridge 1967), no. 369; I.L.S. 28.
4. Tacitus *Annals* XI. 23–25; Michael Grant, *op. cit.*, pp. 49–53.

4

Rome and the Jews

The political background to Jesus's life and ministry was Hellenistic and Jewish, under the remote authority of the Roman emperor. Alexander the Great's conquests had broken down national barriers in what is today called the Middle East, and Greek language and culture were predominant. But there are few signs in the synoptic gospels of Greek or Roman influence until Jesus's arrest, trial, and execution in Jerusalem by the Roman prefect, Pontius Pilate. Provided taxes were paid and there were no violent uprisings, Rome was content to leave effective government to local rulers. Jewish hostility to Rome, however, was a significant and continuous feature of the political background during the first century AD. Not only were the Jews unhappy to be ruled by a foreign power, but the tax burden was heavy, and local tax-collectors, who used to bid for the right to collect, were regarded with loathing as traitors by their fellow-countrymen.

The picture that the gospels paint of life in Galilee is

what one would expect of a remote rural area, with agriculture as its main industry. It fits well the much more detailed account given by the historian Josephus who knew it personally – a mixed pattern of land ownership, large estates alongside small holdings, with the beginnings of a market economy. Josephus also describes the animosity and disdain felt by those who worked and lived in the countryside, in villages and small towns, towards those dwelling in the few large cities. The lively export trade which arose from Galilee's fertility accentuated still further the gap between rich and poor, since it was the already prosperous landowners and businessmen who were its main beneficiaries. As throughout Mediterranean countries in the first century AD, it was a man's world, organized by men for their benefit. Women's role was largely domestic, primarily concerned with looking after the home and the children. Marriages were arranged; almost certainly wives could not divorce their husbands. Since Galileans showed marked loyalty to the Temple in Jerusalem despite their distance from it, pilgrimages to it by devout Jews, for family reasons (Luke 2: 41–52) or to festivals, were regularly undertaken. While Jesus' preaching itinerary cannot be precisely established in the gospels, their various topographical references point to the countryside round the Sea of Galilee (including in particular Capernaum on the north shore) as the main area of his activity.

Jesus's own language was almost certainly Aramaic (Mark 5: 41; 7: 34), but he could probably converse also in Hebrew and possibly in Greek. (Cf. Mark 7: 25–30; John 12: 20–36; Matt. 8: 5–13; Mark 15: 2–5, where Jesus seems to be talking to Greek-speaking persons without an interpreter. In particular, Pilate's question, 'Are you the king of the Jews?', was most unlikely to have been in any language other than Greek. Jesus's reply in Greek, 'You say so', may well have been his actual words.)

Augustus, the first Roman emperor, who ruled from well before Jesus's birth in 5 BC until AD 14, and Tiberius, who succeeded him and was in power until four years after Jesus's crucifixion, left effective control of Palestine to 'client-kings'. The half-Jew Herod, who came to be called the Great, governed Galilee from 47 to 37 BC and, with his brother Phasael, Judaea from 42 BC. Declared king of Judaea by the Roman government in 40 BC, he held Augustus' confidence for many years and was effectively King of the Jews from 37 BC until his death in 4 BC.

These thirty-three years saw three main phases: 37–25 BC during which Herod consolidated his position as he overcame his adversaries who included the Pharisees; 25–14 BC prosperity when his position was secure, during which he built Caesarea on the coast and a palace in Jerusalem, and began to rebuild the Temple (c. 20 BC); 14–4 BC when he was afflicted by severe domestic troubles, largely caused by his ten wives wrangling over the succession.

At Herod's death, Augustus divided his kingdom into three parts, one for each of Herod's three sons, Archelaus, Antipas, and Philip. Archelaus was appointed ethnarch (local ruler) of Idumaea, Judaea, and Samaria; Antipas tetrarch (subordinate ruler) of Galilee and Peraea; Philip tetrarch of Gaulanitis and other parts of north-east Palestine. Archelaus lasted less than ten years, being deposed by the emperor in AD 6 and replaced by a Roman prefect. So Judaea then became part of an imperial province and Jerusalem was under Roman direct rule. Throughout Jesus's life, Antipas (with the dynastic title of Herod) ruled Galilee, and during these years rebuilt the large city of Sepphoris (not mentioned in the New Testament), founded Tiberias as his capital on the west shore of the Sea of Galilee, and in AD 31 or 32 imprisoned and executed John the Baptist.

So far as concerns Jesus, there were only two governmental figures, Herod Antipas, client-king of Rome, and Pontius Pilate, the Roman prefect of Judaea, who for the most part lived in Jerusalem. In the gospels Herod Antipas makes only three appearances: first (Matt. 14: 1–2; Mark 6: 14–16; Luke 9: 7–9), when he expresses a wish to see Jesus since he fears that Jesus might be John the Baptist restored to life; secondly (Luke 13: 31), when the Pharisees warn Jesus against Antipas; and thirdly, when according to Luke (23: 6–12) Jesus is sent to Antipas for trial, just before his crucifixion, a trial which is not mentioned in the other gospels.

As for the Jews, Josephus identifies four main Jewish groups in first-century Judaism: the Pharisees, Sadducees, Essenes, and Zealots, only the first two of which figure to any extent in the New Testament.

There were at least six thousand Pharisees, most of whom were not priests. Though popular and influential, they were not particularly powerful. They were keen students of the collection of divine precepts known as the Torah, strict upholders of the law and keen on legal debate, and guardians of Jewish traditions. They believed in bodily resurrection and final judgement, in free will and divine providence. Jesus shared many of their views, ate meals with them, and sometimes praised them (Mark

12: 34; Luke 14: 1). Where he disagreed with them was over their purity laws, their narrow view of what was involved in keeping the sabbath, their criticism of the company he sometimes kept (Mark 2:16), and their emphasis on the importance of oral tradition in explaining the written Torah.

Associated with the Pharisees, though not identical with them, were the Scribes, professional writers, legal and religious scholars, whom the gospels frequently mention as arguing with the Pharisees against Jesus. They were probably employed by the Pharisees as their legal counsellors (Mark 2: 16; Luke 5: 30). The particularly negative picture that Mark paints of them may be due to the tensions between the early Christian communities and the synagogue Jews. Their appearances in the New Testament are almost all accompanying the Pharisees.

The Sadducees, less numerous and more aristocratic than the Pharisees, differed from them in two main ways: they rejected belief in the resurrection (probably also in angels and demons), and they also rejected the Pharisees' acceptance of oral tradition as being as authoritative as the written Torah. Being Jerusalem's priestly aristocracy, they were chiefly concerned to ensure that the Temple ritual was fully observed, since this helped to maintain the covenant relationship between Israel and God. Thus, since during Jesus's lifetime the High Priests were appointed and dismissed by the Roman prefect, they co-operated with the Romans in the maintenance of law and order, and it is not surprising that the gospels point to the prominent part they played in the negotiations over the trial and execution of one who had so conspicuously attacked the Temple administration.

Of the two remaining Jewish groups identified by Josephus in first-century Palestine, we know a great deal about the Essenes through the Dead Sea Scrolls found at Qumran but very little about the Zealots. Yet, though there were evidently many active Essene communities in Palestine, there is no evidence of any direct Essene influence on, or connexion with, Jesus. The value to us of their preserved writings is in showing how Jesus's teaching would have been understood by his contemporaries in the first century AD.

As for the Zealots, they were once thought to be an active revolutionary movement in first-century Palestine, but recent scholarship suggests that they became prominent only at the start of the Jewish revolt in AD 66–70. That one of Jesus's disciples was called Simon the Zealot may well have meant no more than a personal sobriquet and did not necessarily indicate membership of a revolutionary group. Jesus himself, though wholly committed to the rule of God, clearly did not support armed revolution as a way to achieve his aims.

All these groups shared the fundamental beliefs of Judaism: monotheism (which in the ancient world, where most people believed in many gods, was most unusual); the Jews being God's people, the chosen race as the people of the covenant; and the vital importance of repentance, punishment, and forgiveness. If you sinned, you were punished, but God would forgive you if you genuinely repented. As God's people, Jews saw him active in their history, from the creation story in Genesis, through the founding father Abraham, the exile in Egypt and rescue by Moses (the Exodus), to the establishment of the monarchy, especially of King David, who in the tenth century BC united the kingdoms of Israel and Judah, and was considered subsequently to be a go-between between God and his people. After David, the story became inconclusive. The people of the covenant were moving forwards to a new relationship with God, when he would deliver them from their enemies, but they had not yet arrived and were awaiting a Messiah, another anointed king, to effect this delivery. During the centuries before Jesus, when the Jews lived under foreign domination, they were strengthened by their reliance on God's teaching conveyed to man in the Torah and by the prophets who proclaimed the coming of a new king, David, who would liberate his people and re-establish the kingdom of God. By the first century AD the Jews' hope of deliverance had still not been fulfilled but nevertheless deliverance was still expected. The Roman overlord would be finally thrown out. A new leader, a new teacher, or a new group was sought, who would realize this hope. The expectation of some form of climax to the present world order dominated Jewish thinking and is clearly also seen in Jesus's frequent references to 'the last things', which scholars call 'eschatology'. This should not be taken to mean the end of the universe as we know it, but a dramatic transformation of Israel, the start of a new age when God's kingdom would be fully restored on earth, bringing universal peace and prosperity.

Also central to their world view at this period were the Temple in Jerusalem, their homeland of Israel which God had given them, the Torah, and their racial identity. All aspects of their national life were focused in the Temple, which was thought of as God's dwelling-place. Their country, to which they had been restored after exile, represented the new Eden. The Torah regulated the Temple's activities, and their racial identity was bound up with their religion and culture.

Their three major festivals brought to their memories the key moments in their long history: Passover (the barley harvest) also celebrated the Exodus; Pentecost (wheat harvest) also celebrated God's gift of the Torah on Mount Sinai; and Tabernacles (grape harvest) also celebrated their nomadic period in the wilderness.

Worship of God through holy scripture, which described these events, lay at the heart of their daily existence. In particular the psalter with its praise of God, its thanksgiving, its laments, its royal psalms (which were interpreted as being to some extent messianic) gave ample and moving expression to public and private experience.

Such, in very brief outline, are the main features of the political and religious background to Jesus's ministry. Historically, it cannot be too strongly emphasized, Jesus belongs within Judaism.

5

Historicity of the birth stories

What is clear from even the briefest of studies of the stories about Jesus's infancy is that they are not historical in our sense. How and why were they created, and why did they come to be accepted as true?

Early authentic Christian preaching is to be found in St Paul's First Letter to the Corinthians. Almost certainly written in AD 52–3 within twenty or so years of Jesus's death, when many who had known him and the apostles were still alive, this letter gives a most direct and convincing account of the Last Supper and Jesus's arrest (I Cor., 11: 23–26) and of the resurrection appearances (I Cor. 15: 3–4).

The other instance of early preaching is Luke's account, in Acts, of Peter's first public address, at Pentecost, where he talks of Jesus's crucifixion and resurrection (Acts 2: 23–24, 32). Though Acts was not written until nearly fifty years after the events recorded there, and its author followed Thucydides' practice in composing speeches that were appropriate to the occasion, the detailed account of the Christian community's early origins which it describes has the ring of historical truth. Peter, not Paul, is at that period the leading figure. Some time after his Pentecost address, he cures a cripple outside one of the Temple gates in Jerusalem and gives the credit for his healing power to Jesus whose trial, crucifixion, and resurrection he draws to the astonished onlookers' notice (Acts 3: 14–15; 4.2). Again, after the arrest of Peter and John by the Temple authorities for causing a disturbance, Peter, when examined by the High Priest Annas and others of the high priestly family, claims that the cure of the sick man was due to calling on the name of Jesus whom they had crucified and who had risen from the dead (Acts 4: 10). Later again, some time after Paul's conversion, Peter refers again to the crucifixion and Christ's appearances after his death and resurrection (Acts 10: 39–41).

The emphasis throughout this early evangelism is thus on the crucifixion and resurrection. The detailed description and explanation of the so-called passion, that is the last few days of Jesus's mortal life, which contained so much suffering, was the chief concern of Paul and the apostles. The events that led up to that (the birth, early years, baptism, ministry), although earlier in time, were subordinate and were given narrative form subsequently. In short the gospels were compiled back to front, as indeed was the oral tradition on which they were based. This of course is the reverse of normal biography; and it was done to bring out the significance of Jesus's life which had been understood only partially by the disciples while he was living his human existence. Thus the gospels came to be written in logical rather than strictly chronological order, based on an oral tradition which had grown and flourished in the period of thirty to fifty years after the crucifixion.

Probably the first stage in this development was as set out in Mark's gospel, which is similar to the account given by Peter to Cornelius in Acts mentioned above (10: 37–41). His outline starts with Jesus's baptism by John the Baptist in the River Jordan and ends with the divine messenger's declaration at the tomb that Jesus has risen. There is no mention of Jesus's family background in either account.

By the time at which Matthew and Luke were writing, early Christians had come to want to know who Jesus was, and where he had been born and lived before his ministry. Luke and Matthew may also have thought that they should take account of Jewish criticisms. It is indeed probable that the pre-gospel tradition at least developed in that apologetic direction. How, for instance, could the Messiah have come from Galilee? The two evangelists aimed to answer this question and others by relating what all along could, and should, have been true of Jesus before he entered public life at and after his baptism – namely that his birth, though on the face of it human, had something special about it, that his identity had in some sense been revealed to worshippers outside his immediate family and representing the wider world (Magi, shepherds). The hostile reaction of Herod, described by Matthew, and that mentioned in Simeon's prophecy to Mary that Jesus would later be rejected, are deliberately inserted as matching Jesus's own later experience of acceptance and rejection. The birth stories are in themselves in a sense a preliminary gospel. That this came to be regarded as biographical was a natural consequence of the style in which the two evangelists presented it. Most of the difficulties that we have in trying to harmonize the portrait of Jesus painted by Mark with those of Luke and Matthew can readily be explained when we understand how much later they were written and how far the early Christian oral tradition had developed in the meanwhile.

John's gospel, written still later and in such a different style, is even less biographical. The first event in Jesus's life that he describes is John the Baptist's declaration of Jesus's significance as God's only Son, while the last is the resurrection appearances. He says nothing about Jesus's birth or early years. All the events and sayings that he describes, including the long theological discourses in which Jesus discusses his role, are included in his gospel in order to convince the reader that Jesus is Christ, Son of God. Whether all are historically accurate is less important to John than that they are fundamentally true to the Jesus whom through personal experience and extensive meditation he had come to know.

We can, however, establish with some degree of confidence the date of Jesus's birth, for Matthew's and Luke's dating of it to the time when Herod the Great was still alive is generally regarded as historical (Matthew 2: 1; Luke 1: 5). Herod died in 4 BC and Jesus is thought by scholars to have been born in that year or possibly a year or two earlier. This may seem odd to us as we prepare to celebrate the millennium in 2000, supposedly precisely two thousand years since Jesus was born. The discrepancy is due to a monk's miscalculation in the sixth century AD. Dionysius Exiguus, who came from Scythia (South Russia), lived in Rome, and edited a liturgical

30

calendar which assumed that Jesus's birth was Year One. This calculation was probably based on Luke's two statements (3:1 and 3:23) that John the Baptist, the forerunner of Jesus, began to preach in the fifteenth year of the emperor Tiberius's reign (AD 29) and that Jesus began his ministry when he was about thirty. Allowing a year for John's ministry and assuming that Jesus was exactly thirty when after baptism by John he began his, Dionysius thus made what we call Anno Domini 1 the year of Jesus's birth. This calendar, which ignored Herod's death in 4 BC, became accepted chronology, despite the obvious discrepancy. So it is now generally agreed that Jesus was born about four years B(efore) C(hrist), in 5/4 BC.

The time of year is nowhere mentioned in the New Testament, and 25 December was not regarded as Christmas Day until AD 354. By then this had become recognized as the date of the winter solstice, and was celebrated as the birthday of the Sun God Mithras, to which the birth of Jesus Christ was deliberately opposed.

SOURCES
E. P. Sanders, *The Historical Figure of Jesus*, London 1993, pp. 11–12;
H. Van Soden's chronology in *Encyclopaedia Biblica* (1899);
T. K. Cheyne and J. S. Black, cols. 805 and 807;
J. Finegan, *Handbook of Biblical Chronology*, p. 248.

6

Infancy narratives

O little town of Bethlehem
How still we see thee lie!
Above thy deep and dreamless sleep
The silent stars go by.
Yet in thy dark streets shineth
The everlasting light;
The hopes and fears of all the years
Are met in thee tonight.

* * *

O holy child of Bethlehem,
Descend to us, we pray;
Cast out our sin, and enter in,
Be born in us today.

* * *

Away in a manger, no crib for a bed,
The little Lord Jesus laid down his sweet head.

32

But Jesus was almost certainly not born in Bethlehem, nor in a manger, nor was he visited by three wise men or kings following a star, or even shepherds. The journey to Egypt, and the reason for it, are also hard to defend.

Why are the birth stories unhistorical, and does it matter if they are? The obvious discrepancies between the accounts given by Matthew and Luke, who alone of the four evangelists describe Jesus's birth, are hard to reconcile with each other and with the other two gospels.

Mark (1: 9; 6: 1) and John (7: 41–2) assume that Jesus was born in Nazareth, a small town in Galilee far from the village of Bethlehem which lay some seventy miles south, near Jerusalem. Luke, too, clearly knew of Jesus's association with Nazareth but felt obliged to connect him as closely as possible with David, Israel's heroic warrior king, from whom one who was destined to be the Messiah, Israel's saviour, should be directly descended. So he claims that Joseph, Jesus's father, was descended from David and that he had to return to his ancestral home, Bethlehem, David's city, because of an imperial decree which required all inhabitants to register in their home towns.

There are, however, three reasons why this account is not plausible: first, Luke's genealogy of Jesus is highly suspect (3: 23–38), being almost entirely and strikingly different from Matthew's, as noted earlier (1: 1–17). For instance, Luke has forty-one generations from David to Jesus's birth (3: 23–38), Matthew only twenty-eight (1: 1–17). In this period of a thousand years, only three names (apart from David's and Joseph's) are common to both genealogies. Matthew lists Jesus's forefathers back to Abraham and is concerned to show that Jesus descends from David and is the Davidic Messiah. Luke on the other hand traces Jesus's forebears back to Adam and God, with the intention of showing that Jesus is the Son of God. What is common to both is their determination to connect Jesus to David. Their genealogies are theological rather than historical. This Davidic descent through Joseph might seem hard to reconcile with their assertion that Mary was a virgin, but in accordance with Jewish law it could be transferred through legal not natural paternity. By naming the child, Joseph makes the legal acknowledgement that he is the child's legal father.

Secondly, Luke's story of a decree by the emperor Augustus is also suspect (2: 1–5). There is no reliable historical record of such a general imperial census during Augustus's principate. Galilee at this time was ruled by Herod Antipas, Judaea by Archelaus, and neither country was directly subject to Rome, so a census could not have been held there. The census which Luke records as being held when Quirinius was governor of Syria took place in AD 6 or 7 after Archelaus's deposition when Jesus was at least ten years old. For, as we saw earlier, both Luke (1: 5) and Matthew (2: 1) agree that Jesus was born while Herod the Great was still alive, and we know that Herod died in 4 BC. The historian Josephus, who is particularly well informed on Herod's last years, would certainly have mentioned the census, nor could he have called it, which he dates to AD 6/7, new and unprecedented if there had been one ten years earlier. Luke's ten-year miscalculation is not as surprising as it has often been thought: precisely linked chronologies were not readily available at the time that Luke was writing; what he required was a historical explanation of how a Galilean infant, whose home was Nazareth, came to be born in King David's city. A discrepancy of ten years was relatively insignificant.

Thirdly, Roman censuses were normally held at a man's present home or place of work, not at his birthplace or ancestral home. There was no reason why Joseph, in order to register, should have had to leave Galilee.

As for the evocative story of the manger, which is only to be found in Luke (2: 7), it is possible but unlikely. There were few hotels in the ancient world, Bethlehem was a tiny village, and, if it really was Joseph's home, would there not have been at least one member of his family living there who would have put Mary and him up? In any case why was Mary there? She was in an advanced state of pregnancy, and she was not required to register her name. Would she not have stayed in Nazareth?

Matthew makes no mention of an inn or a manger. He says that Jesus was born in a house (2: 11) in Bethlehem of Judaea and he quotes the prophet Micah (5: 2) as confirmation. This sounds as though it was the home of Joseph and Mary (2: 22). By contrast with Luke who had to find a reason for bringing the holy family from Nazareth to Bethlehem, Matthew has to invent a story for moving the family later from Bethlehem to Nazareth (2: 13–23).

The only other reference to Bethlehem in the New Testament (John 7.40 f.) confirms how unhistorical Jesus's birth there was thought to be. For John describes a discussion among Jesus's contemporaries of his claim to be the Messiah: 'Surely the Messiah cannot come from Galilee. Has he not to be descended from David and come from David's village of Bethlehem?'

Here John makes no attempt to claim that Jesus was born in Bethlehem. The inference is clear: John did not regard it as important where Jesus was born and certainly did not consider that Bethlehem was his birthplace.

What, then, of the Magi, astrologers (translated as wise men in the Authorised Version of the Bible, who in later non-Biblical accounts became three kings) and the shepherds? Are they, too, unhistorical? Matthew's gospel is the only account which mentions that a star heralded Jesus's birth and persuaded the Magi to journey from where they lived in the East to Jerusalem. The story is intrinsically improbable. But a plausible case can just be made, and has been made by Professor Colin Humphreys,[1] which deserves consideration alongside the more likely explanation of the phenomenon.

In classical times a priestly group skilled in astrology, the Magi, who lived in Persia (now Iran), Mesopotamia (now Iraq), and Arabia (now Saudi Arabia) are known to have sent some of their members to visit the rulers of other countries. So such a journey to King Herod the Great by a small party of them is not in itself improbable. Tiridates, for instance, King of Armenia, led a delegation of Magi to pay homage to Nero in AD 66.[2] As for the star, it could only have been a comet. Other descriptions (such as a conjunction of two planets, a meteor, a nova, or supernova) do not adequately account for its peculiar movement through the sky, in particular its stopping over a particular place, Bethlehem. From Chinese astronomical records three comets are identified as appearing at about this time: 12 BC, 5 BC, and 4 BC. The date that fits our other evidence for Jesus's birth is 5 BC, and the Chinese description of this comet's appearance in the east and visibility for more than seventy days accords with Matthew's account. Two months would have been quite long enough for the 550-mile journey from, say, Babylon, the centre of Magi activity, to Jerusalem.

Three unusual astronomical events combined to make the Magi travel to Jerusalem: a triple conjunction of Saturn and Jupiter in the constellation Pisces (7 BC), which happens only every 900 years; a massing of Mars, Saturn and Jupiter in Pisces (6 BC), which occurs only every 800 years; and the 5 BC comet in the constellation Capricornus. The first two events could well have been interpreted to indicate the birth of a divine king, the third that such an event was soon to take place.

Moreover, Matthew's contemporaries would not have been surprised by the star story. The Roman poet Virgil, who lived just before the time of Jesus's birth, tells how his hero Aeneas was guided by a star to the place where Rome should be founded.[3] Julius Caesar was associated after his death with a comet that shone for seven nights at the games which Augustus instituted in his honour. Suetonius[4] reports that a few months before the birth in 63 BC of the future emperor Augustus a portent was seen in Rome warning that nature was pregnant with a king for the Roman people. Tacitus[5] mentions two brilliant comets in Nero's reign (AD 60 and 64)[6] which portended a change of emperor. Suetonius records that Nero consulted the astrologer Balbillus about the significance of the second of them. At the siege of Jerusalem in AD 70 Titus, son of the emperor Vespasian, according to Tacitus[7] saw armies fighting each other in the sky, and the temple in Jerusalem lit by fire from the clouds.

There are, however, good reasons for doubting that this

particular star was historical. First, a comet has a tail, which is clearly visible, and does not look like a single star. Matthew makes no mention of this, nor does it stop over any particular place, as he describes. Secondly, though comets were widely believed to portend future events, these were usually disasters. The comets mentioned by Suetonius and Tacitus during Nero's principate were regarded by the emperor as warnings of his downfall or death.

Moreover, the story as a whole is unlikely. A star that behaved in the extraordinary way described by Matthew would have been most remarkable, but there is no record of it (*pace* Professor Humphreys), historical or astronomical, other than in Matthew. Herod's summons to the priests and scribes for their advice is also hard to accept, for it ignores the hostility that existed between Herod and the Jewish priests. In Matthew's account (2: 4–5) only expert theologians seem to know where the Messiah is to be born, but John (7: 42) describes it as common knowledge that he is to be born in Bethlehem. After the Magi's dramatic visit to Bethlehem, which could scarcely have failed to be noticed in a village of only a few hundred inhabitants, Herod is apparently unable to find out which child had been thus honoured. The account of the Jewish historian Josephus of this period, which deals in detail and at length with Herod's cruel reign, makes no mention of his massacre of all boys in the neighbourhood under the age of two.

Matthew's account of the birth is substantially different from Luke's. Luke does not mention the star, the Magi, Herod, the massacre, or the flight into Egypt and residence there. Instead he has the story of the shepherds and their angelic visitor, and tells of the family's visit to Jerusalem when Jesus was forty days old to be presented to God in accordance with Mosaic law, and their return to their own hometown Nazareth in Galilee (2: 22–40).

To the explanation of these historical problems I shall return. But I must first discuss a much more important and difficult issue, on which Matthew and Luke seem to agree, but which is so miraculous as to be as hard to accept as the resurrection: the virginal conception of Jesus.

NOTES

1. C. Humphreys, *Quarterly Journal of the Royal Astronomical Society*, Vol. 32, 1991, 389–407.
2. Suetonius, *Nero* 13 and 30; Pliny, *Natural History* XXX.vi., 16–17.
3. Virgil, Aeneid II, 694.
4. Suetonius, *Divus Julius* 88; *Divus Augustus*, 94. 3.
5. Tacitus, *Annals* xiv: 22; xv: 47.
6. Suetonius, *Nero* 36.
7. Tacitus, *Histories* V. 13.

7

Virgin birth

That Jesus had no human father but was conceived by his mother through the power of the Holy Spirit is stated in Matthew (1: 18–25) and probably, though not unambiguously, implied in Luke's story of the annunciation (1: 26–38). Mary is surprised at the suggestion that she could become pregnant without sexual intercourse. Matthew evidently thought that the virginal conception was historical though its historical truth was secondary to its theological significance. To Luke, too, the birth story was primarily symbolic. (Virginal conception is a more precise term than virgin birth, since it is not the way that Jesus was born that is our concern but how he was conceived: was there a human father?)

Apart from Matthew and Luke the virginal conception is nowhere else referred to in the New Testament. Some scholars have considered Paul's statement in Galatians 4: 4–5 to be an implicit reference: 'When the term was completed, God sent his son, born of a woman, born under the law...' but what Paul is stressing here is Jesus's humanity, the reality of his birth, not how he was conceived. He makes the same point in Romans 1: 3, 'On the human level he was born of David's stock.' In none of his letters does Paul appear to be in the least interested in Jesus's biographical details. He makes no reference to the birth stories developed later by Matthew and Luke, but his silence should not be taken to indicate that these were not current, if only in embryonic form, during his lifetime.

The silence of the New Testament on virginal conception does not discredit it so much as cast doubt on the view that in the early church it was generally thought to be a fundamental Christian belief.

A more telling argument against it is that Mary did not apparently disclose Jesus's divine origin to his brothers, who in Mark and John are said not to believe in him (Mark 3: 21 with 3.31; John 7: 5). In none of her appearances in the gospels after his birth does she seem to be aware of its significance, or to have communicated this to any of the apostles (Mark 3: 31–5; John 2: 3–4). The resurrection, not the virginal conception, was what convinced them finally that Jesus was the Messiah.

What appears to be definitely historical is the fact that Jesus was born after Mary and Joseph had come together in marriage but some time before the normal period of nine months' pregnancy was complete (Matt. 1: 18; Luke 1: 27; 2: 5–6). Joseph's hesitation over marrying Mary, natural in the circumstances, was overcome by an angelic visitation in a dream. He had decided to set aside the marriage contract but was now persuaded to confirm it. That others, too, thought that Jesus was illegitimate can be traced as early as Mark's gospel (6: 3) where Jesus is

41

called 'son of Mary'. Sons were normally called by their father's name unless their paternity was doubtful. John's gospel (8: 41) also suggests illegitimacy, and this charge is made unequivocally by critics in the second century and thereafter. John relates a fierce argument between Jesus and some Jews who in reply to Jesus's attack that their father is the devil, not God, said: '*We* were not born of fornication.' In the Greek the 'we' is emphatic, so this riposte could be interpreted as a veiled reference to Jesus's own origin. 'Our birth was not illegitimate, but yours was.' John 8: 19 has also been thought to be similarly suggestive. In the second century the charge of illegitimacy was more clearly advanced. The Greek philosopher Celsus, writing an anti-Christian tract in the second half of the century (AD 178–80), imagines what a Jew might say to Jesus: 'Is it not true, good sir, that you fabricated the story of your birth from a virgin to quiet rumours about the true and unsavoury circumstances of your origins? Is it not the case that far from being born in royal David's city of Bethlehem, you were born in a poor country town, and of a woman who earned her living by spinning? Is it not the case that when her deceit was discovered, to wit, that she was pregnant by a Roman soldier named Panthera, she was driven away by her husband – the carpenter – and convicted of adultery? Indeed, is it not so that in her disgrace, wandering far from home, she gave birth to a male child in silence and humiliation? What more? Is it not so that you hired yourself out as a workman in Egypt, learned magical crafts, and gained something of a name for yourself which now you flaunt among your kinsmen?'[1]

Tertullian, the first Christian theologian to write in

Latin, towards the end of this same century told of a Jewish charge that Jesus was the son of a prostitute.[2] Scholars have not found it possible to say whether these later charges of illegitimacy were a response to the gospel stories or an independent tradition. If the latter, they would indirectly confirm Matthew's account.

Matthew himself may have been misled by the Greek translation of the Hebrew word in Isaiah 7: 14 which he quotes as part of the angelic dream's reassurance to Joseph. He sees Mary's pregnancy before sexual mating with Joseph as a fulfilment of Isaiah's prophecy that 'the virgin will conceive and bear a son, to be called Emmanuel, God with us.' (Matt. 1: 23). In the original Hebrew, Isaiah's word *almah* means no more than 'a young woman of marriageable age'. The authors of the Septuagint, however, which was the most widely read Greek translation of the Jewish scriptures, translated this as *parthenos* which Matthew took to mean 'virgin' though classical authors also use it to mean 'an unmarried woman who is not a virgin'. It has been said that the doctrine of the virgin birth might never have been enunciated if this passage from Isaiah had not been misunderstood and misinterpreted by Matthew. But Luke's much fuller and quite different account of the annunciation, which does not refer to Isaiah at all, suggests that the mysterious aspect of Jesus's birth was an early tradition (1: 26–38).

By us, who are so aware of our genetic make-up, Jesus might well be thought to have been more fully human if he had had a human mother *and* father, but this would be to limit God's creative power and to rule out the possibility of miracles.

43

In the last analysis, whether Jesus was conceived miraculously without a human father cannot be decided on the basis of the New Testament. Many scholars have considered the virginal conception as theological dramatisation. Matthew and Luke are not so much concerned to describe a biological miracle as to express their conviction that Jesus's coming into the world involved a special expression of divine prevenience and power. As with other events in Jesus's life we are left to draw our own conclusions from what evidence there is.

In any case whether Jesus was the Son of God does not depend theologically on his relationship to Joseph. The doctrine of the incarnation, that God became a member of his world through his son, does not stand or fall on the historical truth or otherwise of Jesus's virginal conception.

NOTES
1. Origen, *Against Celsus*, I.28, 32, 69.
2. Tertullian, *De Spectaculis*, XXX.3.

44

8

Flight to Egypt? Shepherds?

We saw earlier that Jesus's forebears, as listed by Matthew and Luke, were almost entirely different in each of the two gospels, and that he was almost certainly born in Nazareth, not Bethlehem. The other episodes that Matthew relates which are mentioned neither in Luke nor in the other two gospels, Mark and John, are the flight to Egypt and the reason for it, Herod's massacre of those aged two and under (Matt. 2: 13–23). For his part, Luke alone has the stories of Gabriel's visit to Mary (Luke 1: 26–38); Mary's visit to her cousin Elizabeth, mother-to-be of John the Baptist, and her giving voice to the Magnificat (Luke 1: 39–56); the shepherds' vision of an angel accompanied by a heavenly host which makes them hasten to visit Jesus (Luke 2: 8–20); Jesus's circumcision and presentation in the Temple at Jerusalem (Luke 2: 21–38); and finally, twelve years later, the story of Jesus visiting Jerusalem with his parents for the Passover feast and remaining there after they had left for Nazareth, in order to have discussions with teachers in the Temple (Luke 2: 41–52).

The most reasonable explanation of these differences between Matthew and Luke on the one hand, and between Mark and John on the other, is that the events are not strictly historical in the sense that they actually happened, but that they are an attempt by the evangelists to describe the sort of background to Jesus's childhood that would be appropriate to someone who was later to be revealed as the Messiah. Both Matthew and Luke made extensive use of the Jewish scriptures to establish Jesus's identity as the Son of God, the Saviour of Israel. As is shown by their different treatment of Jesus's genealogies, their aim was to write, not history as we know it, but what has been called salvation history, a presentation of events which portray the essential truth of Jesus as Saviour. Their success in this is clearly confirmed by the long tradition of Christian acceptance of their stories as in a real sense true. Just as other notable figures in history, Napoleon or Churchill for instance, gather stories and sayings about them which may not be historically true but which are true in essence as confirming and illustrating their character as known, so too do the stories about Jesus's birth and early years.

Take Matthew's Egypt story first (Matt. 2: 13–23) as a good example. Luke's account of the holy family's return from Bethlehem to Nazareth and later visit to Jerusalem, when the child was forty days old, conflicts directly with the story of the flight to Egypt. What was Matthew's purpose in including this dramatic story? Note first that about a third of these eleven verses is quotation of passages from the Old Testament. These bring out the parallels with the story of the Jews in Pharaoh's time and their escape from his edict that all Jewish male children should be put to death. As the child Moses was saved from a cruel ruler, Pharaoh, and, when he grew up, led his people of Israel out of Egypt (the Exodus), so Jesus is rescued from the wicked Herod and, emerging from Egypt (Hosea 11: 1), later saves his people. In each story, too, there are other links between the Old Testament and the gospel. There is a Joseph in both, who has a significant dream, and the long quotation from the prophet Jeremiah (31: 15) which describes Rachel weeping in Rama for her children, though less apposite since Rama is not Bethlehem, is intended as fulfilment of prophecy.

Although, as we saw earlier, Herod almost certainly did not massacre the young children, his cruel character is clearly depicted by the historian Josephus.[1] Herod hoped that his soldiers would kill political prisoners so as to ensure that there would be mourning at his funeral. 'All Judaea and every family will weep for me, whether they like it or not.'

In verses 20–21 of Chapter 1 and the first twelve verses of Chapter 2, Matthew portrays the revelation of Jesus as the Christ and its acceptance by non-Jews (virginal conception, star, Magi), and to balance these describes in the second half of the chapter the Jewish authorities' rejection of that revelation and their persecution of Jesus. In his story of Jesus's infancy he combines Old Testament themes with narrative in order to bring out for his own contemporaries his understanding of the gospel. His dramatisation, which gives its message both of triumph and of rejection, has caught the imagination of many who have not perceived its parallel with the cross and resurrection.

Luke also draws extensively on the Jewish scriptures

for his picture of Jesus's early years, from Gabriel's announcement to Mary through the presentation of the baby Jesus (in the Temple at Jerusalem) to Jesus's discussion with the Jewish elders there at the age of twelve.

Consider, first, Luke's story of Gabriel's annunciation to Mary as contrasted with Matthew's equivalent annunciation in Joseph's dream. Whereas Matthew's account draws its material from the stories of the Jewish patriarch Joseph and baby Moses in Egypt, Luke's aim was to portray Mary as representing the lowly and downtrodden, the 'poor' remnant of Israel. The elaborate poetry of Luke's Benedictus, Nunc Dimittis, and Magnificat, so deeply imbued with Old Testament material that it has been called a mosaic of Old Testament and other Jewish writings, was probably non-Lucan in origin, and added by Luke to his own narrative. These canticles, which seem not to be particularly characteristic of those who gave voice to them, could be omitted without loss to the story. Luke, too, follows closely the pattern of annunciations found in the Old Testament. The births of Ishmael (Genesis 16: 7–13), Isaac (Gen. 17: 15–22) and Samson (Judges 13: 3–25) all have identical features – the appearance of an angel, the recipient's fear at the vision, the divine message, the recipient's initial objection, and the promise of a reassuring sign. Moreover, Luke's portrayal of Mary's maternal role is closely modelled on similar portraits in the Old Testament, especially Samuel's mother Hannah (I Sam. 1–2). Yet though both gospels' annunciations are different, both convey to the reader the same essential message, that Jesus is David's son *as well as* God's son conceived through the Holy Spirit.

Next, the swaddling clothes and manger. Luke

mentions the former twice and the latter three times (Luke 2: 7, 12, 16), and calls these a sign. But It is not clear what precise symbolism he wished to suggest. There is possibly a reminiscence of Isaiah 1: 3 where God complains that Israel, his own people, do not know him, whereas the ox knows its owner and the ass knows its Lord's manger. Perhaps Luke's message is that, as the shepherds recognise the Lord when they find him in the manger, so they represent God's people who at last have come to a similar recognition. (The reference to Isaiah would also explain the post-Lucan development of the Christmas story of the presence of animals at the birth.)

As for the shepherds, Luke's equivalent group to Matthew's Magi, their presence may simply be due to their link with Bethlehem, the city of the shepherd David. They represent the many future believers who praise God for what they have seen and heard. Their reaction parallels the praise of God uttered previously by the heavenly host. Just as the Magi depart and are never heard of again in the gospels, so too the shepherds. The memories of adoring worship at Jesus' birth do not reappear at any point in his public ministry. The only link between the stories of the infant Jesus and Jesus' adult life is his mother Mary. By describing her concern for what had happened, Luke points forward to her later discipleship (2: 19–20).

NOTE

1. Josephus, *Bell. Jud.* I.660; *Antiq.* XVII.174–8.

Jesus's baptism and temptation

Although the circumstances of his birth as described in Luke (and only Luke) are probably apocryphal (1: 5–25, 36–37), John the Baptist is without doubt a historical character. Not only does he figure frequently in all four gospels (eighty mentions in all, and nine in Acts) but the historian Josephus also describes him as preaching righteousness and piety, and as executed by Herod Antipas.[1] Almost equally undoubted is his baptism of Jesus. All four gospels give some account of it, with considerable emphasis. In Mark and John, as we saw, it appears in particularly striking expression at the start of their gospels. John the Baptist is portrayed as a forerunner paving the way for a greater figure than himself. Moreover, it is most unlikely that the baptism was a creation of the early Christians since its characteristics did not accord with their understanding of Jesus. Matthew is at pains to explain away Jesus's subordination to John and that John's baptism was a call to repentance and forgiveness of sins (Matt. 3: 11–15; 11: 2–6). The four evangelists nevertheless felt bound to include the episode.

They make the most of the event, the immersion in the River Jordan, the spirit of God descending like a dove, and the voice from heaven, much of which is of course no more than picture language, vivid illustration of the occasion's significance as revealed later. While they accept that John the Baptist is a prophet as well as one who baptises, they make it clear that his baptism is limited to water, whereas Jesus, who is his successor, will baptise with the Holy Spirit and with fire. John the Baptist announces the imminence of judgment and hence calls for immediate repentance, pointing to the hope of restoration. Jesus, though for a period baptising with water, probably as John's right-hand man (John 3: 22–30), does not preach judgement and repentance so emphatically, and after John's arrest by Herod branches out on his own. In finding that he has the power to heal and exorcise, he experiences the kingdom of God as a present reality and stops baptising. John the Baptist's admission that Jesus is mightier than him and is in some sense God's beloved son is confirmed.

The contrast indeed between John the Baptist and Jesus that emerges from the gospels is further evidence of the historical truth of John the Baptist's relationship with Jesus: John is ascetic, Jesus eats and drinks; John practises a baptism of purification and looks to judgement in the near future; Jesus does not stress the need for repentance as much as John and announces that God's reign is already present in his own activities; sinners have only to follow him to be saved. John the Baptist's base was the wilderness; Jesus worked in the towns and villages of Galilee. John wrought no miracles.

51

These differences, which the early Christians recognised as Jesus's divine call, developed after his baptism and temptation, and are counterbalanced by the similarities between the two. Both behaved like Jewish prophets; both led reform movements; both were hostile to the Temple authorities; both had a group of disciples. It is therefore reasonable to accept Robert L. Webb's conclusion[2] that at the historical level John the Baptist was what the early Christians concluded he was at a theological level, the forerunnner of Jesus.

Immediately after his baptism Jesus, we are told by the three synoptic authors (Matt. 4: 1–11; Mark 1: 12–13; Luke 4: 1–13), withdrew to the wilderness of Judaea to prepare for his ministry. There he spent forty days fasting and wrestling with the temptations that would later test his humanity to the full. While the language in which these tests is described is pictorial and much of it not literally true, their essential truth is all the more powerfully conveyed by its mythological and symbolic form. Forty days echoed the forty years spent by the people of Israel wandering in the desert after their exodus from Egypt. Satan, the Hebrew word used by Mark to describe the tempter, had by the first century AD developed from being one of God's advisers in the Book of Job into God's chief spiritual opponent. Matthew and Luke simply call him the devil, but, probably drawing on Q's collection of sayings, give a much fuller and almost identical account of the three temptations.

The first was the devil's suggestion that Jesus should show his divine power by turning stones into bread so as to relieve his hunger. The second was to throw himself down from the pinnacle of the Temple in Jerusalem, trusting that angels sent by God would rescue him. The third was to accept as a gift from Satan all the kingdoms of the world in their glory.

To succumb to each of these would involve subservience to Satan.

To overcome them, Jesus relied on quotations from the book of Deuteronomy (8: 3; 6: 16; 6: 13), each of which can be seen to be relevant to his later ministry.

8: 3 (Man cannot live on bread alone but lives by every word that comes from the mouth of the Lord) has a direct bearing on the feeding of the multitude, suggesting a symbolic significance rather than a supernatural miracle. Jesus is the bread of life to all who believe in him.

6: 16 (You must not challenge the Lord your God). Jesus showed by his later behaviour his reluctance to convince others by sensational miracles or signs.

6: 13 (You shall fear the Lord your God, serve him alone) points to Jesus's frequent reference to the kingdom of God and discussion of its nature. God's kingdom would not be worldly.

Though the temptation stories have such a direct connexion with later events in Jesus's life and his recurrent conflict with evil, and thus might be thought to be simply literary creations rather than historical experience, it is indeed likely that Jesus did prepare himself for his ministry after baptism by a period of withdrawal to pray about the nature of his vocation and the public response to him, and what more appropriate a place to withdraw to than the desert which was where in the Hebrew scriptures one went to meet God?

NOTES
1. Josephus, *Antiq.* XVIII.117–19.
2. Ed. Bruce Chilton and Craig A. Evans, *Studying the Historical Jesus* (Leiden, New York, Köln 1994), p. 229.

10

Jesus's Ministry

Length

As Luke makes clear (chapters 3–4), Jesus began his ministry soon after his baptism by John the Baptist. This took place in the fifteenth year of the principate of the emperor Tiberius (Luke 3: 1). Although there have been different interpretations of this date, it is most reasonable to assume that Luke used the normal Roman method of reckoning. Thus Tiberius' fifteenth year would have run from 19 August AD 28 to 18 August AD 29.

Luke 3: 23 tells us that Jesus was about thirty at the start of his ministry. If, as has been suggested earlier, Jesus was born in 5 or 4 BC, he would have been thirty-three if he began his ministry in AD 29. So that year is confirmed as an appropriate date for its start.

As for the length of his ministry, there have been various theories, ranging from one year to four.

One year, despite the evidence of the synoptic gospels, is most unlikely. Not only would it have been difficult for Jesus in so short a period to have done all that he is described as doing, and to have established the reputation that he did, but John's gospel refers specifically to at least three Passovers (John 2: 13, the first journey to Jerusalem; 6: 4, the feeding of the five thousand; 11: 55, the Passion Passover). These require a ministry of at least two years.

Those, however, who propose a two-year ministry have to transpose chapter 5 and chapter 6 of John's gospel, for which there is no manuscript evidence.

The four-year theory has the main flaw of requiring the addition of an extra year between chapter 10 and chapter 11 of John's gospel, for which there is no evidence in the gospels.

It is, then, most reasonable to conclude that Jesus's ministry extended at least over three years, starting in the summer or autumn of AD 29 and ending at the Passover of AD 33. This would require an additional year between the two Passovers of John 2: 13 and 6: 4, but such is suggested by John 4: 35 and 5: 1, the latter referring to a Jewish feast other than Passover.

Thus a possible outline of the events of his ministry would cover three and a half years:

1st year – AD 29 (summer or autumn) to April 30, the first Passover of his ministry, not a full year.
2nd year – Passover 30 to Passover 31.
3rd year – Passover 31 to Passover 32.
4th year – Passover 32 to Passover 33.

In the first year we may place the forty days' fasting and temptation in the wilderness (forty being a symbolic number indicating a long time, as in the Flood), the disciples' first call, the wedding feast at Cana, followed by his visit to Capernaum and journey to Jerusalem (John 2: 12–13). The second would include activity in Jerusalem, Judea, and Galilee, and the imprisonment of John the Baptist. In the third year the Galilean ministry continues, with much healing effected, the twelve apostles are sent out and return, and news of John the Baptist's death reaches Jesus. The fourth year sees Jesus retire from public ministry and withdraw with his disciples to Phoenicia. Thereafter, apart from a possible visit in September to take part in the Feast of Tabernacles, he returns to Galilee to continue teaching and healing until he goes up to Jerusalem to face his trial and death.

Chronology
A possible chronology of Jesus's life is thus established as follows:

5/4 BC	Born.
c. AD 8 (April)	Visit aged twelve to the Temple in Jerusalem.
AD 29	Baptised by John the Baptist. Begins ministry.
30 (April)	Passover in Jerusalem.
31 (Oct.)	At Feast of Tabernacles in Jerusalem.
32 (April)	Second Passover of ministry in Jerusalem.
(Sept.)	At Feast of Tabernacles in Jerusalem.
(Dec.)	At Feast of Dedication in Jerusalem.
33 (March–April)	Final week in Jerusalem.
	28 Sat. Arrives in Bethany; 'Mary' anoints.

29 Sun. Thronged by crowds.
30 Mon. Triumphal entry into
    Jerusalem.
31 Tues. Curses fig-tree; cleanses
    the Temple.
 1 Wed. Challenged in Temple;
    discourse on Mount of Olives.
 2 Thurs. Last supper, betrayal,
    and arrest.
 3 Fri. Trial and crucifixion
    (Nisan 14).
 4 Sat. In the tomb.
 5 Sun. Resurrected.

11

Jesus's titles

A study of the three titles applied to Jesus in the New Testament (Messiah, Son of God, Son of Man) does not make clear how Jesus regarded himself or his relationship to God. For the gospels and Acts use all three in different ways at different times.

The Son of Man, for instance, found only in the gospels and on Jesus's lips (except for Acts 7: 56 by Stephen at his death and in Heb. 2: 6 and Rev. 1: 13; 14: 14), often simply means a person or the first person, I. 'Foxes have holes, and birds of the air have nests, but the Son of Man has nowhere to lay his head' (Matt. 8: 20) means no more than 'I have no home'. A second context where the title also means I is the thrice repeated prediction of his death and resurrection (Mark 8: 31; 9: 31–2; 10: 33–4, matched by similar references in Mark and Luke). If this is historical, it is surprising that his disciples understood it only after his crucifixion. A third meaning is one who, coming with the clouds of heaven, will establish the kingdom of God on earth (Matt. 16: 27–28; 24: 30–31;

59

Mark 8: 38; Luke 9: 26). This is based on the vision of the prophet Daniel (7: 13–14):

> I saw one like a son of man coming with the clouds of heaven; he approached the Ancient in Years and was presented to him. Sovereignty and glory and kingly power were given to him, so that all people and nations of every language should serve him; his sovereignty was to be an everlasting sovereignty which should not pass away, and his kingly power such as should never be impaired.

Jesus's apparent reference to this prophecy (Mark 13: 26) in relation to himself has been understood by many scholars as claiming the messianic role of final deliverer of Israel. In a similar description Paul, writing to the Thessalonians (I Thess. 4: 16) much earlier than the gospel authors, uses the word Lord rather than Son of Man. At his trial, however, while appearing to accept the titles of Christ and Son of God, Jesus seems to refer, less than directly, to his role as the Son of Man who will be exalted at his coming (Matt. 26: 63–64; Mark 14: 62), so we cannot be sure how Jesus thought of this title. His varied use of it may have been deliberately designed to give expression to the mysterious nature of his mission and himself. Some scholars, however, consider that it was the early church that developed the significance of this title and applied it to the risen Christ as expressing the essence of their faith.

The Son of God, a title applied to Jesus by all four gospels, is also indeterminate. What it did not mean to Jesus's Jewish contemporaries was a half-human, half-divine hybrid. There were many Greek myths about such divine creations current in the first century (Zeus, for example, in the shape of a swan impregnating Leda and siring two children by her). The birth stories are often mistakenly thought to convey such a meaning but Jews thought of themselves as children of God in the sense that they were all God's creation as described in the Old Testament. The writers of the gospels applied the title in the singular, directly or indirectly, to Jesus in several contexts: his baptism, his temptation, his transfiguration, his trial, his death, at exorcisms of demons, and at Peter's confession. They do not define the title with any precision but appear to use it to indicate Jesus's special status, not that he is only half-human. By the time that they were writing, it had become accepted practice, as Paul's Letters, written a generation earlier, show, to associate the title Son of God with that of Christ, Messiah. Mark opens his gospel (1: 1), John concludes his (20: 31) with such a declaration. To John in particular, Jesus Christ was at one with God (1: 1), and to him this is what Son of God had come to mean. But Jesus himself, because of the Jews' firm belief in a single God, would not have thought of himself as divine (Mark 10: 17–18). It is notable that it is mainly in John's gospel that Jesus uses this title of himself, even though he clearly felt a special relationship with Israel's God, on several occasions called him Father (for example, Matt. 11: 25–27; Luke 10: 21–22), and at his trial before the Sanhedrin appears to accept the title of Son of God to some degree in all four gospels.

Messiah is a much more complex title, with a long and varied history in the Old Testament. The Hebrew from which it comes means simply 'anointed' (which Greek translates as *christos*), and is applied to priests, prophets, and kings. It did not indicate divinity. To first-century

Jews, as we saw earlier, Messiah meant primarily Deliverer or Saviour, and the Messianic hope included the restoration of King David's throne, the overthrow of the Roman empire, the return of the exiled people of Israel, the renewal of the Temple in Jerusalem, and the establishment of the kingdom of God. The early Christians saw Jesus as King David's descendant, anointed by God for the task of restoring Israel. Hence his birth in David's city. But he proved not to be the expected warrior-king. His reign was established through his role as suffering servant, not by force of arms. His kingdom was not fully established, but simply embryonic. So, although his followers came to see him as Messiah, he was not the Messianic figure that they had expected from their understanding of the Old Testament.

How far Jesus thought of himself as the Messiah it is hard to be sure. When John the Baptist sent two of his disciples to ask him who he was, his reply, quoting Isaiah 29: 18–19; 35: 5–6; 61: 1 which conveyed glowing pictures of the Messianic age, could be understood as his acceptance of the Messianic role and title (Matt. 11: 2–6; Luke 7: 18–23). When asked at his trial whether he was, the synoptic gospels give two different responses: In Mark he said 'Yes, I am'; in Matthew and Luke his reply is equivocal. He acted, however, in his ministry as clearly a man with a mission, a mission which both concerned the whole of the land and the community of Israel and at the same time was designed to elicit a personal response from individuals. His mission, of which he presumably became aware at his baptism by John, was to proclaim the reign of God and do all he could to bring about the restoration of Israel. He saw himself as fulfilling definitively their hopes as their new king.

N. T. Wright[1] argues forcefully, and at length, that Jesus saw himself as more than this, as the long-expected Messiah, but with a redefined purpose. By what he said and did he showed himself to be the representative of the people of YHWH (Yahweh), coming to 'bring about the end of exile, the renewal of the covenant, the forgiveness of sins.' Satan, and all that Satan stood for, not Rome, was the enemy. He chose twelve apostles to match the twelve tribes of Israel, with three of whom he had, like King David before him, a specially close relationship. His eating and drinking with a wide social range of people symbolized the openness of the messianic banquet. The authority and significance of his teaching and preaching were messianic. If Jesus had not seen himself as Messiah in this sense, and had not, at least to some extent, explained his understanding of his redefined role to his disciples, why did the earliest Christians attach the word Christos to themselves so soon after his death? Jesus's crucifixion was not enough by itself to have a Messianic meaning unless such a meaning was already inherent.

But this is surely to discount the overwhelming revelation that the resurrection and the subsequent meetings with the risen Jesus must have had on the disciples. Moreover in general the view that Jesus was fully aware that he was the Messiah accepts too readily the thrust of the evangelists' message which we need to remind ourselves was a post-resurrection development.

As for the so-called Messianic secret, namely that Jesus deliberately kept his identity as Messiah secret until shortly before his death because he did not wish his Messianic status to be understood by any but committed believers, this may conceivably have a more profound explanation, namely that Jesus, being fully human, only became completely aware, at the final point of his earthly life, when as a human being he died, of who precisely he was, of the special characteristics of his Messiahship, of his divine nature. This would explain his restrictive attitude to the title of Messiah at Caesarea Philippi (Mark 8: 27–30) when, in reply to his question who did the disciples think he was, Peter said 'The Messiah'. The concept of the Messiah being a suffering servant of humanity was so different from the traditional view of a kingly deliverer that it is not surprising that it took time for it to be understood. In only that one episode, Peter's forthright declaration, is Jesus's demand for silence a specific reference to his Messiahship.

There are, however, many occasions where the evangelists make no attempt to conceal what could be called the messianic character of Jesus's sayings or actions (for example, the feeding of the Five Thousand, Matt. 14: 13–21; Mark 6: 32–44; Luke 9: 10b–17; John 6: 1–15).

In other episodes (for instance, when Jesus is hailed as Son of David by the blind beggar Bartimaeus), it is the onlookers, not Jesus, who try to silence him (Matt. 20: 29–34; Mark 10: 46–52; Luke 18: 35–43).

The contrast between secrecy and publicity is a frequent feature of Jesus's ministry as described in the gospels, and serves to emphasise his special authority rather than his Messiahship.

NOTE
1. N. T. Wright, *Jesus and the Victory of God* (London 1996), pp. 528–39.

12

Miracles

How far can the many miracles attributed to Jesus by the four evangelists be regarded as in any sense historical? That they bulk large in the gospels, and are a highly characteristic part of his ministry, is clear: with the omission of parallels and of his conception and resurrection, the gospels give accounts of thirty-three that Jesus performed, and there are a further ten texts which summarize his miraculous acts. So questions about these require an answer. Did Jesus perform miracles? If so, what form did they take? Are any of them based on genuine reminiscence rather than on early Christian creativity and insight? If indeed he performed miracles, what was his purpose in doing so?

Before attempting to answer these questions, we would do well to consider the first-century attitude towards miracles. In the ancient world, miracles were accepted as supernatural phenomena, often due to some god's activity. Recourse, for instance, was often had to the Greek god of healing, Asclepius, whose main shrine was at

Epidaurus in the Peloponnese, just as the sick visit Lourdes today. Where doctors failed, or were thought to have failed, the sick would pray to a god for a miraculous cure. The spread of belief in Asclepius's healing power is evidence enough that many who prayed to him or visited one of the many shrines dedicated to him, were restored to health and were ready to acknowledge this. Today we know that spontaneous remission of even lethal disease can occur and that, in general, healing often takes place naturally without, or despite, medical attention. The ancients did not differentiate, as we would, between illnesses or deficiencies that were impossible to cure, such as loss of a limb, and those where it was reasonable to look for a cure. Stories of amazing cures abounded, and people did not query whether they were true or false.

Others beside the gods were thought to perform miracles, the most famous of these being Apollonius of Tyana who lived at the same time as Jesus and was for a period better known. There were also Jesus's Jewish near-contemporaries such as Hanina ben Dosa.

So where today we tend to look for a rational explanation of events that surprise us and do not believe in miracles, the ancients, including the early Christians, were not so inhibited. The historian Josephus, for instance, believed in miracles such as the Israelites crossing of the Red Sea, and even heightened the miraculous element in the story of Daniel and Nebuchadnezzar, but he also on occasion looked for a rational explanation. Jesus's disciples certainly thought he had remarkable powers and with many other spectators were astonished by what he did.

Nevertheless, of the four types of miracle with which

Jesus is credited – healing and exorcism, revivification, nature, and missionary – the first of these causes least difficulty to almost all scholars. Even the arch-critic, R. Bultmann, who believes that very little of the gospels is historically true, is willing to accept that Jesus was a healer, and there are many scholars who believe that a number of the healing stories are indeed based on early reminiscences of the disciples: the healing of Peter's mother-in-law (Mark 1: 29–31), the healing of blind Bartimaeus (Mark 10: 46–52), the healing of the man with the withered hand (Mark 3: 1–6), the healing of the leper (Mark 1: 40–45), of the paralytic (Mark 2: 1–12), of the woman with the haemorrhage (Mark 5; 25–34), of a blind man at Bethsaida (Mark 8: 22–26), of the centurion's son at Capernaum (Matt. 8; 5–13), and the exorcism of the epileptic boy (Mark 9: 14–29). All these accounts are notable for their vivid description and detailed location as from a first-hand witness.

So most scholars accept that Jesus was a remarkable healer, and that as such he cured many sick people and exorcised many demons. During his ministry this is a sphere of activity which, as the many examples in the four gospels show, he made very much his own, often attributing his power to the faith of those who came to him for help or insisting on the forgiveness of the sufferer's sins as a prior requirement. In particular, the repeated accusation of the Pharisee critics (Mark 3: 22–30) that Jesus's power to exorcise demons comes from Beelzebub, the prince of demons, is especially noteworthy for Jesus's reply: 'If I cast out demons by Beelzebub, by whom do your sons cast them out?... But if it is by the finger of God that I cast out demons, then the kingdom of God has come upon you.' This was a definite claim that through his healing power he was inaugurating God's kingdom. There was no reason for such a controversy to be recorded unless it was true.

Furthermore in the second century the stern critic of Christianity, Celsus,[1] and some possibly independent Jewish sources refer to Jesus's reputation as a healer.

Of all the miracles, those associated with healing and exorcism are the easiest for modern man to accept as historical. Similar, if less dramatic, healing has taken place from time to time down the ages and continues up to the present. Psychosomatic explanations are today accepted as genuine.

Much harder to accept as historical are the three miracles of revivification from death: Jairus's daughter may not have been dead, simply unconscious, so this could come into the healing category (Mark 5: 21–43). But there is no such plausible explanation of the bringing back to life of the widow's son at Nain (Luke 7: 11–17) or of Lazarus at Bethany (John 11: 1–44), particularly the latter with its grim description of someone who has been dead for over three days. That each of these last two stories occurs in only one gospel increases one's scepticism, and belief in their historicity is still further weakened when the evangelists' purpose in placing them at a particular point in their narrative becomes clear. Luke's story parallels the similar revivification of a widow's son by the Old Testament prophet Elijah (I Kings 17: 17–24). The miracle is not concerned with faith but with showing Jesus's compassion. It leads appropriately to Jesus's answer to John the Baptist's disciples which comes next in his narrative (Luke 7: 18–23). As we saw in the last chapter, they came to ask whether Jesus was the Messiah, he who is to come, and Jesus's reply was to point to his healing achievements: 'the blind receive their sight, the lame walk, the lepers are clean, the deaf hear, the dead are raised to life, the poor are hearing the good news.' This was confirmation from the prophet Isaiah (29: 18–19; 35: 5–6; 61: 1) of Jesus's authenticity. The early Christians would not have been troubled by whether the miracle of revivifying the widow's son had taken place; they certainly believed that Jesus could raise and had raised to life those thought to be dead. Though Pliny the Elder,[2] a contemporary historian, denied that God could recall the dead or give mortals immortality, his was not a typical view, and there are several other similar stories in the first century of the restoration to life of a dead person (for example, the miracle recorded by Philostratus as performed by Apollonius of Tyana).[3]

The raising of Lazarus can be explained similarly. Only John mentions it, and his account is detailed and resonant with echoes of Jesus's own resurrection: Lazarus has been dead three days; he is buried in a rock-tomb at Bethany; Thomas's characteristic intervention; the part played by Mary; the linen bands round his body and the cloth round his face; two disciples invited to come and see; his loud cry to Lazarus like his cry on the cross; the episode designed for the glory of God, in which God's son will also share. Lazarus's return to life indeed points forward to Jesus's death and leads directly to it; the Sanhedrin's resolution to condemn Jesus arises from this event. Jesus by his action shows the depth of his love for his friends, and reveals himself as the resurrection and the life. But only those who believe are able to grasp that Jesus can, and has, overcome death.

As for the so-called nature miracles – the calming of the storm on the lake (Mark 4: 35–41), the feeding of the five thousand (Mark 6: 30–44) and four thousand (Mark 8: 1–10), Jesus walking on the water (Mark 6: 45–52), the withering curse of the fig-tree (Mark 11: 12–14, 20–26), the coin in the fish's mouth (Matt. 17: 24–27), the wine transformation at Cana (John 2: 1–11) – these seem to us today much less convincing and more akin to legend. Only the disciples witnessed most of them; most have parallels in the Old Testament or contain motifs from it; they do not form part of Jesus's public ministry, and they are not associated with any of Jesus's magisterial pronouncements. Finally, they represent and promote the beliefs of the early Christians, and so are likely to have been developed in the early oral tradition.

The development of these stories into accounts of miracles can with some plausibility be explained rationally. For instance, Peter's failure to copy Jesus and walk on the water points to his later failure of nerve at Jesus's trial when he denies his association with him; Jesus's taming of the storm is more likely to be a story to comfort the early Christians when they were passing through troublesome times of political oppression; the feeding of large crowds is perhaps best explained by a symbolic interpretation, foreshadowing Jesus's presidency at the sacramental meal of the eucharist.[4] A similar sacramental interpretation has been applied to the water becoming wine at the wedding party at Cana. If Jesus had really

used these two occasions as miraculous interference
with the laws of nature, he could, with some reason, have
been criticized for giving in to the first of the three
temptations which he had rejected in the wilderness at
the outset of his ministry.

Finally, what did the earliest Christians think was
Jesus's purpose in performing miracles? It is generally
agreed that his mission was to promote his belief in the
reign of God (reign rather than kingdom because the
latter implies location, whereas the former indicates
activity). This reign was to him both present and future
– present, as revealed by the power of his activity as a
healer, teacher, and worker of miracles, and future
because it was not yet established universally and still
met with much resistance. Jesus was seen by many to
be a charismatic teacher, given power by God to work
miracles as part of his mission. But his miracles could
only be fully effective for those who had faith in him, and
many did not have that faith. So his miracles, particularly
those of healing and exorcism, helped to create on the
one hand an enthusiastic, if small, band of disciples from
among those who found his miracles impressive, and, on
the other, opponents from among those who preferred
to regard him as a magician and sorcerer, and did not
accept his claim to be God's agent.

But even his closest followers, the apostles, did not
grasp, during his earthly life, his full significance. That he
was inaugurating a new reign of God they came to believe
only after the resurrection.

NOTES
1. B. Chilton, *op. cit.*, p. 361; Origen, *Against Celsus*, I.6, 28, 38, 68; II.9, 14, 16, 48–9; III.27; V.51, 57; VI.77.
2. Pliny the Elder, *Nat. Hist.* II.v.27.
3. Philostratus, *Vita* IV.16.
4. Cf. Mark 6: 41–2 with Mark 14: 22.

13

Aphorisms and parables

Jesus was a great charismatic teacher, publicly, albeit improperly, called Rabbi (Master) in his lifetime, the substance and style of whose teaching was essentially similar to those of Jewish Rabbis but was more demanding, authoritative, and controversial. He taught almost entirely by personal example or in vivid parables, the message of the former often conveyed in short didactic statements or aphorisms, most of which are so distinctive that they can be regarded as almost certainly historical, such as: 'Love your enemies; a prophet will always be held in honour, except in his home town, and in his own family; pay Caesar what is due to Caesar, and pay God what is due to God; it is not the healthy that need a doctor, but the sick.'

As Theissen and Merz make clear,[1] many of these pithy pronouncements tell us much about Jesus's social relationships. His relation to his family is discussed later (pp. 89–90) but his reply to the question put by John the Baptist's disciples (Matt. 11: 2–19) and comment on it confirm in succinct language his view of John the Baptist's preaching which we considered earlier (pp. 51–2).

His relationship to his disciples, to those who stayed faithful to him is well illustrated by his brisk summons to Simon and Andrew, and to the sons of Zebedee, to abandon fishing and follow him (Mark 1: 16–18, 19–20), and in his description of the reward for loyal discipleship: 'No one who has given up home ... for my sake and for the Gospel, will not receive ... a hundred times as much ... and persecutions besides...' (Mark 10: 28–31).

His sympathy with women and respect for them are also striking characteristics, unusual in an androcentric society, as is most movingly illustrated by his defence of the woman who anointed him in Bethany with expensive ointment, a scene that is described in some detail in all four gospels (Matt. 26: 6–13, Mark 14: 3–9, Luke 7: 36–50, John 12: 1–8).

His dealings with his opponents (also discussed briefly on pp. 86–8) are sharply illustrated by his responses to his opponents' criticisms, such as his rebuke to the Pharisees, 'The Sabbath was made for man and not man for the Sabbath', and his comment to the Sadducees on the resurrection, 'God is not God of the dead but of the living' (Mark 12: 26–7).

Parables, however, were his chief teaching instrument, that is, if we except John's gospel and if parables are defined as widely as possible as picture language designed to illustrate some aspect of behaviour or belief. More narrowly defined as extended similes, stories, or allegories, parables are infrequent in John. Instead of stories illustrating God's relationship with people (for example, the Prodigal Son, the Wicked Husbandmen of the Vineyard) John describes Jesus using symbolic discourses based on a single striking analogy: I am the Bread of Life (6: 35), I am the Light of the World (8: 12), I am the Door of the Sheep (10: 7), I am the Good Shepherd (10: 11), I am the Resurrection and the Life (11: 25), I am the True Vine (15: 1), I am the Way, the Truth, and the Life (14: 6). Scholars agree that these two very different styles of teaching were not used by Jesus concurrently, and that the teaching method used by the historical Jesus is most likely to have been that which is represented in the synoptic gospels. Yet there are nine sayings in John's gospel which mirror Synoptic sayings (for example, 'Destroy this temple, and in three days I will raise it again.' John 2: 19 and Mark 14: 58). What, however, we find only in John's gospel is the essence of Jesus's teaching, in profound theological language, as understood by the evangelist after years of deep reflexion (John 16: 13, 25).

Most scholars believe that the synoptic parables are unquestionably among the most characteristic and authentic sayings of Jesus, and this is confirmed by their unmistakably Palestinian, even Galilean atmosphere. So it is no surprise that a great deal of modern theological discussion centres on them, and that they raise many questions to which there is as yet no agreed answer: for instance, how far is Jesus's original message faithfully conveyed by the evangelists? How unique is it? How far do Rabbinic parallels shed light on the parables? How subversive and unconventional are they? How limited to particular contexts? What ethics, theology, or Christology can we legitimately derive from them? Why does Mark assert that Jesus spoke in parables to conceal his meaning from the crowds who listened to him?[2]

It may nevertheless be said, with some confidence, that several parables show their Jewish provenance and their place in the Jewish prophetic tradition: shepherd and sheep, and vineyard, represent in the Old Testament the King of Israel and Israel itself; master and steward, father and son, are found in contemporary Jewish parallels to picture God and his people. But Jesus adapted what he found and gave such stories a new and provocative slant. They are, too, subversive to the extent that they were essentially critical of the prevailing view of the nation's identity and hopes, and often in cryptic language point to a new dispensation. In them Jesus shows himself to be 'the prophet of judgement and renewal.'[3]

Such a message, if preached too openly, might have caused undue controversy too quickly, so that, as Mark plausibly suggests, Jesus chose to express it in domestic pictures drawn from everyday life in Galilee, and explain the inner significance privately to his closest disciples.

The view used to be widely held that most parables had only one central point and that their details were for illustration and had no special significance. In recent years this view has been modified and scholars now accept that several parables (not only the Soils and the Sower's Seed) should be interpreted allegorically with explanation of the main details. In particular, many of Luke's parables contain several theological truths, not simply one. Indeed in most of his narrative parables Jesus usually makes three points. Allegorical interpretation, however, should as a rule be limited to the main characters, and in general each parable should be related to

76

its original Jewish setting in Palestine of the first century
AD and to Jesus's teaching as a whole. We need to ask
what particular audience Jesus was addressing and in
what circumstances? Further help towards understanding the parables is gained by looking to the end of each,
by considering closely passages of direct speech, and by
noting which character or theme has most emphasis.

An analysis of the thirty or so main parables reveals
that only five are found in all three synoptic gospels[4] (the
Soils and the Sower's Seed, the Mustard Seed, the Wicked
Husbandmen, the Divided House, and the Fig-tree's
Growth), a further six[5] are found in Matthew and Luke
(the Leaven, the Marriage Feast, the Lost Sheep, Wise and
Foolish Builders, Wise and Foolish Servants, Talents), and
twenty, among which are some of the best known and
best loved, in one gospel only.[6] Only one of these (the
Secret Growth of the Seed) is found in Mark; only
Matthew has the stories of the Unforgiving Servant, the
Generous Employer, the Wise and Foolish Maidens, the
Sheep and Goats;[7] Luke alone has the Good Samaritan,
the Unjust Steward, the Rich Man and Lazarus, and the
Prodigal Son, the last of which has been more fully dis-
cussed than any of the others.[8]

It is clearly significant that the theme of the five
parables found in all three synoptic gospels, and in many
of those found in only one or two gospels, is that of the
kingdom or reign of God. This indeed is the central theme
of Jesus's sayings with his implicit, and only partly understood, claim to deity. There are, however, real difficulties
in regarding all parables in their present gospel form as
fully historical. To take one example only, Matthew's final
comment at the end of his story of the labourers in the

vineyard (the last shall be first and the first last) does not fit the sense of the narrative which implies that all in the kingdom of heaven will be equal. Such difficulties of interpretation as remain suggest that either Jesus's original teaching was not always fully understood by his disciples, or that the oral tradition did not tell it with complete accuracy, or that the editorial composition of the gospels introduced minor alterations which had been developed by the first Christian communities. Nevertheless a critical analysis of Jesus's parables, expressed in such striking language as they are, suggests that almost all have at least a kernel of historical truth. The pictures that they convey so vividly had their origin in some words of Jesus, and their meaning may well have been different in different contexts. Hence the discrepancies in the synoptic gospels.

What, then, is the reign of God to which so many of the parables refer?

NOTES
1. G. Theissen and A. Merz, *The Historical Jesus* (Gottingen 1996), p. 193.
2. Ed. Bruce Chilton and Craig A. Evans, *Studying the Historical Jesus* (1994), pp. 253–4.
3. N. T. Wright, *Jesus and the Victory of God* (London 1996), p. 180.
4. The Soils and the Sower's Seed: Matt. 13: 3–8, Mark 4: 3–8, Luke 8: 5–8.
The Mustard Seed: Matt. 13: 31–32, Mark 4: 30–32, Luke 13: 18–19
The Wicked Husbandmen: Matt. 21: 33–44, Mark 12: 1–11, Luke 20: 9–18
The Divided House: Matt. 12: 25–26, Mark 3: 24–26, Luke 11: 17–18
The Fig-tree's Growth: Matt. 24: 32–36, Mark 13: 28–32, Luke 21: 29–33

5. The Leaven: Matt. 13: 33, Luke 13: 20–21
The Marriage Feast: Matt. 22: 1–14, Luke 14: 15–24
The Lost Sheep: Matt. 18: 12–14, Luke 15: 4–7
Wise and Foolish Builders: Matt. 7: 24–27, Luke 6: 47–49
Wise and Foolish Servants: Matt. 24: 42–51, Luke 12: 35–48
Talents: Matt. 25: 14–30, Luke 19: 12–27
6. The Secret Growth of the Seed: Mark 4: 26–29
7. The Unforgiving Servant: Matt. 18: 23–35
The Generous Employer: Matt. 20: 1–16
The Wise and Foolish Maidens: Matt. 25: 1–13
The Sheep and Goats: Matt. 25: 31–46
8. The Good Samaritan: Luke 10: 25–37
The Unjust Steward: Luke 16: 1–8
The Rich Man and Lazarus: Luke 16: 19–31
The Prodigal Son: Luke 15: 11–32

14

The kingdom or reign of God

The kingdom of God (or, in Matthew, of heaven), as described by Jesus, is an elusive expression. That it occurs so often in the synoptic gospels (Matthew has fifty-five references, Mark twenty, Luke forty-six) in so many different contexts is the reason for this.

To the Jew Jesus it would, as we saw earlier in the discussion of his titles, have had many Old Testament overtones, of the re-establishment of David's kingship under the rule of God, of the restoration of the twelve tribes of Israel to their kingdom, of the return of a golden age of peace, plenty, and justice, when the days would be spent in celebratory banqueting. To many if not most of Jesus's contemporaries this kingdom would have been a military and political achievement, a victory over their present rulers. Jesus, however, thought of this restoration and celebration as symbolic of an ideal community created by God, not as a state established by men's force of arms. His disciples did not apparently grasp this: hence John's and James's wish to sit beside him in his kingdom.

What more did Jesus wish to convey about the kingdom? A study of his many references to it, of his many parables, with their rural, domestic, and social similes – such as good seed, yeast in flour, discovery of hidden treasure, a huge catch of fish, vineyard workers all earning the same wage despite different length of service, invitations to a great supper – show many different strands in his thinking, but in most the ideal community of the kingdom, when God's chosen people are restored to a full relationship with him, is only attainable in the future, but a future that is imminent. There are, however, three passages where it is possible to suppose that Jesus saw in his *present* actions some adumbration of the kingdom, some suggestion of what it might be like in practice. In Luke 17: 20–21, when asked by the Pharisees when the kingdom was due, Jesus replied that the kingdom of God was not coming with signs to be observed but was already in their midst. In Matthew 12: 28 (and Luke 11: 20) he suggests to his disciples that his casting out demons by the power of the Holy Spirit shows that the kingdom of God has come upon them. Lastly, as we saw earlier, Matthew 11: 2–6 and Luke 7: 18–23 picture Jesus replying to John the Baptist's disciples' inquiry whether Jesus was the Messiah: 'the blind recover their sight, the lame walk, the lepers are cleansed, the deaf hear, the dead are raised to life, and the poor are hearing the good news.' While in one sense this is no more than a claim to be fulfilling Isaiah's promises (Isa. 29: 18–19; 35: 5–6; 61: 1), it was also a tactfully indirect suggestion that the kingdom of God was present in his ministry. God's rule was being established by healing the sick and preaching to the poor.

As for the kingdom's definition in the future, there are three main distinctions: first, it is there now in heaven, but entry to it comes only after death, and then only if earned by good behaviour in this life (Mark 10: 17–22). Secondly, God will one day bring his kingdom into this world and transform society. The Lord's Prayer is the best illustration of this hope: 'Your kingdom come, your will be done' (Matt. 6: 10; Luke 11: 2). Thirdly, God's rule will be established on earth by the Son of Man, accompanied by disturbance in the heavens, darkened sun and moon, and stars falling – in sharp contrast to Luke 17: 20 above (Mark 13: 24–27; Matt. 24: 29–31; Luke 21: 25–28).

That this prophecy about the dramatic intervention of the Son of Man into this world was never fulfilled and that thus Jesus was mistaken in his prediction has disturbed many from earliest times. The first Christians not unreasonably assumed that Jesus's reference to the coming of the Son of Man referred to himself, and therefore expected his return in power soon after his resurrection. As the years passed without that return they had to revise their understanding of his message. Can we today by a study of Jesus's sayings on this subject grasp what he really thought? That he envisaged a divine intervention by the Son of Man in the immediate future seems certain. The many references to this unfulfilled prediction would have been edited away by the evangelists if it had been possible to do so. Such intervention would have involved a process of judgement by which some people would be allocated to heaven and others to hell. That such a view is probable is confirmed by the preaching of John the Baptist who urged his listeners to repent because the kingdom was at hand (Matt. 3: 1–2). As God had personally and dramatically helped Israel in the past, for instance at the time of the exodus from Egypt, so in the last days he would intervene again, in some final manifestation of power, to create an ideal society. This society John probably regarded as ideal, not because it was a political or economic settlement, but because those who were its members were those who had responded to his teaching. That Jesus's prophecy was unfulfilled in the form he described could be considered evidence of his full humanity.

This belief of Jesus gave his teaching that sense of urgency which is so characteristic of it. The promise of the kingdom was a call to action here and now; only by immediate repentance, humbling oneself before God, was entry into it possible; response in the present ensured membership of the kingdom in the future.

It has, however, been suggested that Jesus's call to repentance was perhaps not quite as important a part of his message as his emphasis on God's love for mankind, a suggestion that has some force. For though all the synoptic gospels attribute the word 'repent' to Jesus, it is much more prominent in Luke than in Matthew and Mark, and it is not mentioned in John. Jesus did not preach the same message as John the Baptist whose call to repentance was much more urgent and demanding. God's love and mercy, said Jesus, are available; he forgives rather than judges and avenges; the kingdom is at hand. The parable of the lost sheep as presented in Matthew 18: 12–14 and in Luke 15: 3–7 brings out the difference of emphasis. If one sheep in a man's flock of a hundred went astray, he would go and search for the one which was lost and leave the rest to look after themselves.

In Matthew this is to give expression to God's love for individual sinners: 'It is not the will of my father who is in heaven that one of these little ones should perish.' Luke's conclusion differs: 'There will be more joy in heaven over one sinner who repents than over ninety-nine righteous persons who need no repentance.' Matthew emphasizes God's search, Luke the sinner's repentance. The good news that God's love is freely given is more likely to transform men and women than a stern injunction to repent or else. God is as much merciful Father as Lord.

To show that this love was for all, whatever their background, Jesus taught that it was available to the weak, afflicted, and despised, even to those who were not Jews. Bad characters, tax collectors, cripples, the deranged and sick, Roman soldiers were all potential beneficiaries. Meals shared in fellowship with all sorts of people were a distinctive part of his ministry. Acceptance of God's gracious forgiveness was the first step to restored health. Jesus brought love's saving power to all who responded to his teaching.

Prayer
Much of this power Jesus claimed came from prayer. Luke reports his praying at his baptism (3: 21–2), before selecting the twelve apostles (6: 12), praying alone in his disciples' presence (9: 18), at his transfiguration (9: 29), and teaching his disciples, at their request, how to pray (11: 1–4; Matt. 6: 9–13). But it is not clear whether the so-called Lord's Prayer originated as a single prayer spoken by Jesus, was developed by later liturgical reflexion from Jesus's prayer in Gethsemane, was a series of

separate petitions edited by the early church into a single prayer, or even what language it was first spoken in.

Matthew (6: 5–6) tells of Jesus urging them to pray always in private. Matthew and Luke, as we saw earlier, describe in some detail Jesus's temptation in the wilderness, which, following his uplifting baptism by John, was clearly a profoundly prayerful struggle over his identity and purpose (Matt. 4: 1–11; Mark 1: 12–13; Luke 4: 1–13). Mark also describes his going very early in the morning to a lonely place to pray (1: 35), and later (9: 29) gives Jesus's explanation why his disciples had failed to heal the epileptic boy: only prayer could effect such a cure.

Jesus's faith in the efficacy of prayer he further describes in 11: 24. All three synoptics emphasise the intensity of his prayer in the garden at Gethsemane shortly before his arrest (Matt. 26: 39; Mark 14: 35–36; Luke 22: 42–44). In short, prayer was such a characteristic activity of Jesus's ministry that there is no reason to doubt that the importance and power of prayer are unquestionably historical aspects of his message.

15

Conflict

While scholars continue to disagree over how precisely Jesus understood his mission, it can be reiterated with some confidence that he directed it to all the people of Israel. He not only proclaimed the coming of God's reign but also set himself to bring it about. He saw himself as effecting the final and definitive fulfilment of Israel's hopes. The activity through which he aimed to elicit Israel's faithful response he described variously as gathering the flock, bringing the law to completion, searching for the lost sheep, inviting sinners to the banquet of salvation, curing the sick, healing the disabled, casting out devils, and restoring the dead to life.

Jesus's teaching and actions, based on his profound self-belief, inevitably caused conflict and controversy. Though some scholars have argued that such stories were probably a late development of the early church as Christians sought to distinguish their life-style from that of the Jews, a comparison of the controversies described in the gospels with those discussed by Paul suggests that the former can safely be related to Jesus during his lifetime. Chapters 2 and 3 of Mark (2: 1–3: 6) provide a sharp summary of these stories: the healing of the paralysed man, preceded by Jesus's announcing that his sins were forgiven, which outraged the lawyers present; Jesus's call of a tax-official to discipleship, followed by his sharing a meal with him and other bad characters; and his signal rebuff to his Pharisee critics, 'It is not the healthy that need a doctor, but the sick'; Jesus's explanation of why he and his disciples did not fast when the Pharisees and John's disciples did; his statement on how the sabbath should be regarded; and, lastly, his cure, in a synagogue on the sabbath, of a man in the congregation who had a withered arm. These were each occasions of apparent conflict with those who regarded themselves as in some sense authorities on the behaviour expected of devout Jews.

N. T. Wright[1] has argued to some effect that where conflict occurred, it was because of Jesus's eschatological beliefs and agenda. Jesus did not speak against the law; indeed he quoted two Old Testament texts (Deuteronomy 6: 4–5, Leviticus 19: 18) with approval as being the two greatest commandments: love God wholeheartedly, and your neighbour as yourself. But he also claimed that the law did not in all respects go far enough. In the so-called Sermon on the Mount (almost certainly not spoken on a single occasion, but a collection of Jesus's sayings compiled later by the evangelists) he was not proposing that the commandments should be repealed, but that Moses's code should be extended. Love your enemies (Luke 6: 27–28), for instance, was a radically new extension of traditional Jewish teaching. The climax of Israel's history was at hand, with major unexpected consequences for

Israel's national life. Jesus's view of Israel's destiny and vocation differed markedly from that of the Pharisees. God was even now bringing in this redefined reign through Jesus. Such an overwhelming claim by Jesus, a message of total love, was not surprisingly the core of the criticisms of Jesus's Jewish contemporaries. Arguments about how to keep the sabbath, about the food laws, about the Temple, were the surface expression of that deep fundamental conflict.

NOTE
1. N. T. Wright, *op. cit.*, e.g. pp. 91–8.

16

Challenge to family?

Two particular aspects of Jesus's teaching that seem to have been especially controversial relate to the family: first, his sharp challenge to family loyalty, and secondly, his views on divorce.

The three sayings on the family, whose striking originality confirms their historicity, are 'Leave the dead to bury their own dead' (Matt. 8: 21–2; Luke 9: 59–60), 'Who is my mother? Whoever does the will of God' (Matt. 12: 46–50; Mark 3: 31–35; Luke 8: 19–21), and his reply to the woman who said 'Blessed is the womb that bore you', 'Blessed rather are those who hear the word of God and keep it' (Luke 11: 27–28) Compare also Jesus's stern warning on the conditions of discipleship (Matt. 10: 37–38; Luke 14: 26–27.)

These evidently shocked those who heard them and, if taken at their face value, justifiably so. Jewish family loyalty was strong, based on the Mosaic commandment to honour father and mother, and these sayings of Jesus were not only personally most challenging but also, as N. T. Wright has suggested,[1] subversive socially, culturally, religiously, and politically. That his rejection of family ties was reciprocated by his own family is most likely have been true since Mark would have omitted, if he could, an episode so apparently damaging to Jesus's reputation.

It is, however, reasonable to accept that what Jesus was trying to indicate was the urgency of the need to follow him in his drive to establish the reign of God. There was no time to fulfil the normal obligations of family piety. To respond to Jesus's summons to follow him was more immediately important to the disciple who asked for leave to attend his father's funeral than burying his father. That could be left to other members of his family. Jesus was making clear that loyalty to himself and his mission created an alternative family, which was open to all who understood its *raison d'être* (Matt. 19: 29; Mark 10: 29–30; Luke 18: 29–30). This was the ideal community which he urgently aimed to create.

What he meant by his teaching on divorce is less clear, not least because of different accounts in the synoptic gospels of what he said.

What we can assert on this topic is that discussion of divorce between Jesus and the Pharisees is almost certainly historical. Not only are there four references in the synoptic gospels, but Paul's first letter to the Corinthians, written more than ten years before the earliest gospel, refers to Jesus's view. 'To the married I give this ruling,' wrote Paul (I Cor. 7: 10–11), 'which is not mine but the Lord's: a wife must not separate herself from her husband; if she does, she must either remain unmarried or be reconciled to her husband; and the husband must not divorce his wife.'

Whether Matthew's view (5: 31–2; 19: 3–9) that Jesus allowed divorce in the case of unchastity is historical is much less certain. Not only does it conflict with the other two synoptic accounts (Mark 10: 2–12; Luke 16: 18) which disallow divorce in all circumstances, but it does not accord with the perfectionism that is typical of so much of Jesus's other teaching. Jesus in quoting Genesis 1: 27 and 2: 24 in response to the Pharisees' quotation of Deuteronomy 24: 1–4 is asserting that divorce runs counter to God's plan for human beings and is only allowed in Moses's dispensation because of human weakness.

NOTE
1. N. T. Wright, *op. cit.*, p. 278.

17

Jesus's supporters

A man's quality and value can often be assessed, at least
to some extent, by looking at those with whom he
consorts. So a study of Jesus's disciples should contribute
to our understanding of him.

There is no reason to doubt that their nucleus consisted
of young fishermen, but we are told very little more about
them. What we learn of their characters, personalities, and
interests comes from the accounts of their various
responses to Jesus's challenges and activities. The gospels
even differ over what might seem to be a straightforward
matter of fact, the names of those closest to him. Only
seven apostles are named in all four gospels: Simon Peter,
Andrew his brother, James and John sons of Zebedee,
Philip, Thomas, and Judas Iscariot. The names of four
more are found in the synoptic gospels and Acts:
Bartholomew; Matthew (also called Levi), James son of
Alpheus, and Simon the Zealot. Three others are also
called apostles: Judas not Iscariot (son of James, named
by Luke, John, and Acts), Thaddaeus (mentioned in Mark

and Matthew, and in Matthew called Lebbaeus by the New English Bible translators), and Nathanael (who appears only in John).

Thus there are fourteen names for the Twelve Apostles. What is the historical explanation of this apparent discrepancy? It is probable that the figure should be regarded as symbolic, not factual. The Twelve Apostles represent the Twelve Tribes of Israel, and the number symbolized Jesus's aim to effect the full restoration of Israel as the new people of God. That Twelve was symbolical rather than strictly numerical is further confirmed by Paul's reference to the Twelve after the resurrection. Paul, writing years before the evangelists, was describing Jesus's appearances after the treachery of Judas had reduced the number of apostles by one to eleven.

Of those apostles who make some individual mark, Peter is by far the most conspicuous. From his first introduction to Jesus by his brother Andrew, when Jesus tells him that he will be called Peter the Rock, to Jesus's final command, 'Follow me', at that historic picnic on the shore of the Sea of Tiberias, Peter's impulsive eagerness, his instant recognition of Jesus's inner significance, his possessiveness and self-assertion, mingled with wavering loyalty, are notable characteristics. Other apostles are less striking: Andrew, who in addition to introducing his brother to Jesus is always mentioned in his brother's company; John and his brother James, ambitious and pugnacious; doubting Thomas who needs to see for himself before he believes; and Simon the Zealot, whose sobriquet may indicate membership of a revolutionary party or, more likely, suggest an enthusiastic nature. *If* he was a member of such a party, he is the only apostle who can be regarded as, in any sense, having a political affilia-tion. There is no evidence to support the theory of those who have argued that Jesus and his apostles were politi-cal revolutionaries.

Beyond the Twelve we are told of three groups of sup-porters: women, who accompanied him on his journeys through Galilee (Luke 8: 1–3) and who were the only loyal spectators brave enough to be present at his crucifixion; seventy-two disciples, less close to Jesus than the apostles but faithful enough to be despatched by him on a missionary enterprise (Luke 10: 1–12). Since only Luke mentions the Seventy and records Jesus's charge to them in similar terms to his charge to the Twelve (Luke 9: 1–5; Matt. 10: 5–42), it must be doubted whether such a group existed and took part in a separate missionary journey during Jesus's lifetime. Seventy is a symbolic number in the Old Testament (for instance, in Numbers 11: 16–17 seventy elders were appointed to help Moses), and Luke may simply have wished to draw attention to the fact that in the early church many other disciples than the Twelve took Jesus's message to non-Jews.

Lastly, there were a few rather shadowy persons, some named, who had sympathy with Jesus but not enough to be counted as his disciples, such as Nicodemus and Joseph of Arimathea.

18

Transfiguration

To what extent was the transfiguration of Jesus a historical event? While John's gospel contains no narrative account of it and chooses instead to show how Jesus's whole life was glorious, it was clearly an important episode in the synoptic gospels, as its vivid description in Mark (9: 2–10), closely copied by Matthew (17: 1–9) and Luke (9: 28-36), makes clear. All three agree that it took place in the presence of Peter, James, and John, Jesus's closest friends who were later with him in the garden at Gethsemane, that it followed a precise number of days after Peter's dramatic declaration near Caesarea Philippi (that Jesus was the Christ) and Jesus's subsequent rebuke of Peter when he could not accept that such a role would involve Jesus's suffering and death. All three describe Jesus's metamorphosis, his glittering white appearance on a mountain side, accompanied by Moses and Elijah who converse with him, Peter's offer to make three booths or tents, the overshadowing cloud, the voice saying, 'This is my beloved (in Luke, 'chosen') Son, listen to him,' and the disappearance thereafter of Moses and Elijah. This voice from an unseen source clearly recalls the similar voice heard at Jesus's baptism and also has some resonance with the manifestation of the infant Jesus to the Magi.

There are also many symbolic Old Testament references: for instance, Elijah's role as forerunner to the Messiah, the temple in Jerusalem likened to a tent, the cloud as indicating God's presence, Jesus's face shining like Moses's when he met the Lord on Mount Sinai.

Both Matthew and Luke, however, do more than simply repeat the Marcan account; they both adapt it to bring out the episode's significance as they saw it. For Matthew, Jesus invites the disciples so as to reveal the Son of Man's glory when he comes to rule. The presence of Moses and Elijah indicates the witness of the law and the prophets to Jesus's fulfilment of Old Testament expectations. Luke's use of the unusual word exodus for Jesus's death points to Jesus's accomplishing a new 'exodus' in Jerusalem, replacing the traditional exodus from Egypt, a new liberation from bondage replacing the earlier.

Mark's placing of the episode immediately after Peter's declaration is all part of his editing the early church tradition that, while Jesus was alive, the disciples failed to understand the concept of Messiah as Jesus understood it. Historically, then, if the transfiguration happened at all, if it holds more than a symbolic meaning as contrasting those who believe and accept Jesus's divine status with those who regard him as a remarkable human being, it was *either* some form of illuminating experience of the three disciples before Jesus's death whose profound significance they only grasped later in the light of the resurrection, *or* a post-resurrection appearance which early tradition placed before the resurrection as being more appropriate to the gradual unfolding of the disciples' understanding of Jesus's identity. For if Peter, James, and John had been present at such an amazing and revealing event as early in Jesus's ministry as is suggested by the synoptic gospels, why were they so demoralized by his crucifixion?

19

The crucifixion: when?

Jesus's crucifixion was a definite historical event and its date can be established with some certainty. We know from Roman sources, historical and inscriptional, that Pontius Pilate, who ordered Jesus's execution, was Prefect of Judaea from AD 26–36.[1] We know, too, that Caiaphas, the High Priest who condemned Jesus, was High Priest from about AD 18–37. Luke dates the start of Jesus's ministry to AD 29. In his gospel John mentions three different Passovers (2: 13, 23; 6: 4; 11: 55–12: 1), so Jesus's ministry, as we saw earlier, is likely to have extended over more than two years. The chronology of Paul's career fits best with a crucifixion date in the late twenties or early thirties AD. Thus most scholars now agree that Jesus was crucified between AD 29 and 33. (A few, on the basis of events concerning the death of John the Baptist and the marriage of Herodias to Antipas as narrated by Josephus, place the crucifixion in AD 36, but the order of events in Josephus's account is not strictly chronological and; unless this is so, the conclusion as to the later date is unsound.)

Even greater precision is possible:all four gospels state that Jesus died shortly before the start of the Jewish sabbath, that is before nightfall on a Friday. According to the Jewish calendar the Passover festival, the most popular of the three pilgrimage festivals held each year in Jerusalem, was always held on 14 Nisan (the name of the Jewish month falling in our March/April); so the synoptic gospels, which place the crucifixion on the day *after* Passover, place it on Friday 15 Nisan, while John's gospel, which places it also on a Friday, places it *on* 14 Nisan, the day *of* the Passover. In which years between 26–36 did 14 Nisan or 15 Nisan fall on a Friday?

Reconstruction of the Jewish calendar of the first century AD is not easy because it is lunisolar, the years being divided into months reckoned by phases of the moon. These years were thus only twenty-nine or thirty days long and produced a year of 354 days. So every two or three years a thirteenth month had to be added (intercalated) to bring the lunar years into line with the solar year of 365 days. While most years, then, were 354 days, some were 383 or 384 days long. A further complication arises from the way in which the start of each lunar month was calculated. The Jewish calendar was established by astronomical observation, not simple calculation, and this observation involved identifying the first faint glow of the crescent moon just after sunset, Jewish days thus beginning in the evening. If weather conditions were adverse and the moon was hidden by cloud, a month could well begin a day late. (This occurred only rarely because Jerusalem, being surrounded by desert, had mostly cloudless nights.)

One final complication relates to the date of Passover.

In fixing this the authorities had to take account of the weather, for Passover was a spring festival and was immediately followed on 15 Nisan by the festival of Unleavened Bread when the first fruits of barley had to be offered in the Temple. If bad weather had held the crops back or if the lambs were too young, a leap-month would have been intercalated. However, it has been calculated that during the decade 26–36, if Nisan had on any occasion been one month later, 14 Nisan would never have fallen on a Friday and 15 Nisan would have fallen on a Friday only in 34.

So it has been established that the only astronomically and calendrically possible dates for the Friday crucifixion during 26–36, for 14 Nisan are 11 April 27, 7 April 30, and 3 April 33, and for 15 Nisan 23 April 34. (14 Nisan in 36 fell on Saturday, 31 March, a further argument against this year for the crucifixion. 15 Nisan might also have been on 11 April 27 instead of 14 Nisan because of atmospheric conditions.)

AD 27 is too early, preceding the date established earlier for the baptism of Jesus as being 29; and 36, for reasons given, may be ruled out of consideration. If Paul's conversion is dated to 34, as many scholars agree, this would rule this date out for the crucifixion. Even if Paul was converted two years later in 36 as I proposed earlier, 34 is only possible as a date for the crucifixion if the weather was particularly poor.

So these considerations suggest that Jesus was crucified on 14 Nisan, the day of the Passover, as John indicates (18: 28; 19: 31), coinciding with the slaughter of the Passover lambs. This is consistent with the chronology given by Paul in his First Letter to the Corinthians (I Cor.

5: 7; 15: 20). His picture of Jesus as the sacrificed Passover lamb and the first fruits of the harvest of the dead matches John's.

With the crucifixion established as being on 14 Nisan, the only two possible dates for it are AD 30 and 33. The latter fits the literary evidence best. The reference in John 2: 20 to the forty-six years spent building the Temple at Jerusalem makes it likely that the first Passover of Jesus's ministry was in 30, and Pilate's vacillation at Jesus's trial would be more intelligible after 31, in which year the emperor Tiberius ordered provincial governors not to maltreat the Jews. The gospel references to Pilate 'not being a friend of Caesar' (John 19: 12) and his new friendship with Herod Antipas, tetrarch of Galilee, after Jesus's trial fit the historical context of 33 better than 30.

It has been further argued that a lunar eclipse, which can graphically be described as the moon turning to blood, was mentioned by Peter in his speech at Pentecost, seven weeks after the crucifixion. He quoted the prophet Joel as confirmation of what had happened at the time of Jesus's crucifixion and resurrection: 'The sun will be turned to darkness and the moon to blood before that great and glorious day of the Lord shall come.' (Acts 2: 20.)

If this speech is historical, the passage can readily he understood as referring to Good Friday and the resurrection, the moon being turned to blood describing a lunar eclipse on the evening of Jesus's death. A similar occurrence is also described in an apocryphal fragment (Report of Pilate) which states that 'at Jesus's crucifixion the sun was darkened ... the moon appeared like blood.' An astronomical analysis of lunar eclipses visible from

Jerusalem between AD 26–36 produces only one such at Passover time, namely on 3 April 33.[2-6]

So the Last Supper was not a Passover meal, but a meal that was so close to the Passover that it seemed to the apostles very much like one, and it is almost certain that Jesus was crucified on 3 AprilAD 33 at the age of 37–8.

NOTES

1. V. Ehrenberg and A. H. M. Jones, *Documents Illustrating the Reigns of Augustus and Tiberius* (London 1976), p. 369; Josephus, *Antiquitates Judaicae* XVIII.55–89, *Bellum Judaicum* II.169–77; Philo, *Legatio*, 299–306.

2. J. K. Fotheringham, *The Evidence of Astronomy and Technical Chronology*, Journ. Theol. Stud. xxxv (April 1934), pp. 146–62.

3. Harold W. Hoehner, *Chronological Aspects of the Life of Christ* (Grand Rapids: Zondervan (1977), pp. 95–9.

4. J. Finegan, *Handbook of Biblical Chronology* (Princeton 1964), pp. 285–301.

5. Colin J. Humphreys and W. G. Waddington, *Dating the Crucifixion*, Nature, vol. 306, No. 5945 (22 December 1983), pp. 743–6; *Astronomy and the Date of the Crucifixion*, Chronos, Kairos, Christos: Nativity and Chronological Studies Presented to Jack Finegan, Ed. J. Vandaman and E. M. Yamauchi (Indiana 1989), pp. 165–81.

6. George Ogg, *The Chronology of the Public Ministry of Jesus* (Cambridge 1940), pp. 261–77.

20

The crucifixion: why?

Similarity of gospel accounts
If the date of the crucifixion is reasonably clear, it is more difficult to discern with confidence why Jesus did what he did in his last week as a human being and why the authorities executed him. What is clear is the outline of events as described by all four authors of the gospels, whose accounts, despite their different authorship and provenance, are remarkably similar.

1. Jesus's triumphal entry into Jerusalem on a donkey: Matt. 21: 1–9; Mark 11: 1–10; Luke 19: 28–40; John 12: 12–19. All four gospels refer to him as son of David or king.

2. Jesus cleanses the Temple by driving out the money-changers and stall-holders: Matt. 21: 12–13; Mark 11: 15–17; Luke 19: 45–46; John 2: 13–17 (though he places the episode much earlier in Jesus's ministry).

3. Later, in the nearby village of Bethany, Jesus is anointed by a woman: Matt. 26: 6–13; Mark 14: 3–9; John 12: 1–8. Cf. also Luke 7: 36–50.

4. Jesus foretells his betrayal: Matt. 26: 21–25; Mark 14: 18–21; Luke 22: 21–23; John 13: 21–30.

5. Jesus has his last supper with his disciples; he breaks bread and drinks wine with them, saying that he will not drink wine again until he drinks it in the kingdom of God: Matt. 26: 26–29; Mark 14: 22–25; Luke 22: 15–20; John 6: 51–58 (indirectly).

6. During the last supper Judas Iscariot leaves in order to betray him to the chief priests: Matt. 26: 14–16; Mark 14: 10–11; Luke 22: 3–6; John 13: 2; 13: 27.

7. Jesus withdraws with the Eleven to the garden at Gethsemane in the Kidron valley between Jerusalem and the Mount of Olives, and there prays: Matt. 26: 36–46; Mark 14: 32–42; Luke 22: 39–46; John 18: 1; 12: 27.

8. Jesus, betrayed by Judas Iscariot, is arrested there by a posse of the High Priest's guards: Matt. 26: 47–56; Mark 14: 43–52; Luke 22: 47–53; John 18: 2–12.

9. Jesus is questioned during the night by the Sanhedrin (though probably not all if its members) in the High Priest's house. He is unsuccessfully accused by false witnesses of having threatened the Temple's destruction: Matt. 26: 57–68; Mark 14: 53–65; Luke 22: 54–71; John 18: 13–24. Mark alone says that, when the High Priest asked, 'Are you the Christ, the Son of the Blessed [i.e. God]?' Jesus said, 'I am.' Matthew and Luke give Jesus a non-committal reply to the same question: 'You say so', which the High Priest takes as an admission. No gospel reports him denying the title. For all four evangelists the trial before the Sanhedrin ends with the decision that Jesus must be put to death.

10. In the morning Jesus, now a convicted criminal, is led, bound, to Pilate's headquarters and tried by him:

Matt. 27: 1–2; 11–14; Mark 15: 1, 2–5; Luke 23: 1, 2–5; John 18: 28–38. Pilate asks him whether he is king of the Jews and according to the synoptic writers he gives a non-committal reply: 'You have said so.' In John's gospel he admits it but says that his kingdom is not of this world. It is not political.

11. Finally, in order to satisfy the Jews who demand Jesus's crucifixion on the grounds that he is a political threat, Pilate, though apparently not considering Jesus guilty, hands him over to the soldiers to be crucified: Matt. 27: 24–26; Mark 15: 15; Luke 23: 24–25; John 19: 16.

What was the significance and truth of Jesus's three actions, the triumphal entry into Jerusalem, the cleansing of the Temple with which is associated his prediction of its destruction, and his behaviour at the Last Supper? What motivated the High Priest to arrest Jesus and insist on his execution by Pilate, the Roman procurator? Why did Pilate give way?

The triumphal entry into Jerusalem

> Rejoice, rejoice, daughter of Zion,
>   Shout aloud, daughter of Jerusalem;
> for see, your king is coming to you.
>   his cause won, his victory gained,
> humble and mounted on an ass,
>   on a foal, the young of a she-ass.

> Zechariah 9: 9

The references in the gospels of Matthew and John to Zechariah's Messianic prophecy (9: 9) give the clue to the

105

meaning of Jesus's gesture in entering Jerusalem on a donkey, on the Sunday before the Passover festival.

He was symbolically declaring his kingship and simultaneously establishing its untypical character, of humility in triumph. The verse in Zechariah (9: 10) following the one quoted by the evangelists emphasizes the peaceful nature of the king's rule. The gospels' suggestion that this demonstration was hailed by a large crowd is almost certainly an exaggeration. Although at Passover, one of the three great feasts of the Jewish year, Jerusalem was packed with many thousands of excitable pilgrims, the Roman and Jewish authorities would have been on the lookout for trouble and Jesus would have been arrested five days earlier than he was if his claim to kingship had been as widely supported as the gospels suggest. Some scholars have even queried whether this incident took place at all, and have argued that it was a development, like the birth stories, of early Christian tradition. But the synoptic writers have included so much strange suggestive detail that the story seems more likely to have been essentially historical, though on a much smaller scale. Jesus's instruction to his disciples on how to find his mount, entry into Jerusalem on a young ass, hitherto unridden, rather than on foot (which in itself was some sort of claim to sovereignty), the spread of garments and branches on the road, the crowd's cries of Hosanna, and the mention of King David – all combine to confirm historicity.

The Temple – cleansing and prediction of destruction
To the Jews their Temple in Jerusalem was of pre-eminent importance, for it was where their God was supposed to

dwell. As such and as the place of sacrifice, it was the central religious and political symbol of Judaism. There God's presence was daily celebrated, and worshippers whose fellowship had been broken by sin could have this restored. Jesus's attitude to the Temple, however, is not easy for us to discern, though it clearly so much alarmed the High Priest Caiaphas that it led to his almost immediate arrest. In driving out those who were making the Temple a market, he is said by the synoptic writers to have quoted Isaiah ('My house shall be called a house of prayer' 56:7) and Jeremiah ('But you have made it a den of robbers' 7: 11). From these remarks, whether he made them or not, or whether they were added later by the evangelists as being appropriate, it looks as if Jesus's attack was another symbolic gesture, demonstrating his authority as a prophet while expressing his objection to the Temple authorities' corrupt ways and his desire to see the administration reformed. Restoration rather than destruction seems to have been his aim.

But the synoptic authors also state that in this last week of his earthly life he predicted the destruction of the Temple and that this prediction was widely enough known for him to have been charged at his trial, as well as on the cross by passers-by, with threatening to destroy the Temple. Since, however, in Acts we see the apostles continuing after the crucifixion to take part in Temple worship, and Jesus's general attitude to Jewish law was to complete rather than abolish it, it seems most unlikely that Jesus threatened to destroy it. It is much more likely that he was urging its reform and at the same time predicting that, unless that happened, it would ultimately be destroyed. John's placing of the threat in a different context, at the start of Jesus's ministry, just after his first miracle at the wedding in Cana-in-Galilee, points to a second and more profound interpretation: 'Destroy this temple,' said Jesus, 'and in three days I will raise it again.' To us now, as to John's contemporaries, these words had a double meaning and were a forecast of his resurrection.

The Last Supper

Jesus's actions at his last supper are his third and final symbolic gesture in this dramatic week. Although, if we accept John's rather than the synoptic account, it was not a Passover meal (John 13: 1; 18: 28; 19: 14), it was so close to the Passover festival that it had much of its flavour of a sacrificial meal commemorating Israel's liberation from Egyptian oppression.

There is no suggestion anywhere in the New Testament that a paschal lamb was eaten, as would have happened if it had been a Passover meal. Instead we have four accounts, almost identical, one of which was written by Paul less than twenty years after the event (I Cor. 11: 23–25), much earlier than the gospels. The only significant difference between them is that Paul and Luke (Luke 22: 18–20) state that Jesus called the cup of wine the new covenant in his blood, whereas Matthew (26: 28) and Mark (14: 24) say that Jesus called the wine his blood (of the covenant), poured out for many. It is not unreasonable to interpret this discrepancy: Jesus was saying that the wine poured out, representing his personal sacrifice, was establishing a new bond between him and his followers. His outpoured blood would effect the redemption and forgiveness of all who came to accept him. In place of the old covenant between God and Israel, which is fundamental to Old Testament religion, this new covenant between God and man was made perfect by his life and death.

At the same time, by his vow (Matt. 26: 29; Mark 14: 25) not to drink wine again until he could drink it in his father's kingdom, he was making a solemn declaration that the kingdom was near and that he would soon be part of it.

Thus all the symbolic gestures of Jesus's last week were later seen by his disciples as his calling attention to the new kingdom of God in which he would have the key role. This would be open to all believers.

Why was Jesus arrested?
Jesus was arrested in an olive grove lying in the valley of the river Kidron between the city of Jerusalem and the Mount of Olives. Is this true and, if so, why?

It has been suggested by some scholars that Caiaphas, who as High Priest was responsible to the Romans for the maintenance of law and order, feared an assault by Jesus and an armed band of his followers. But this is too extreme an interpretation of events; if it had been a real threat, Jesus would not have been the only person tried and executed. His disciples would also have been arrested.

But clearly Jesus posed some sort of threat at a most sensitive time of the year when Jerusalem was crowded with visitors for the Passover festival: the dramatic attack on the Temple market stalls must have offended many and was enough in itself to alarm Caiaphas, for the Temple was such a sacred institution. He had probably also heard at second hand, if not directly from Judas, of

Jesus's triumphal entry into Jerusalem when his entourage and some of those present in the crowd had hailed him as king. That Jesus's view of the coming kingdom was altogether different, and not narrowly political, would not have been known. So Jesus must have seemed a real threat, and he was not unaccompanied. He and his small band of followers might start a riot. Thus it was only prudent to send an armed guard to arrest him in the place to which he had withdrawn with a few of his closest friends.

This is the story that the gospels tell, and there is no good reason to suppose that at this point they are not completely historical. The incident of the anonymous disciple who fled naked from the garden points to an eyewitness account (Mark 14: 51–52).

Why was Jesus executed?
There are two questions to be answered: Why did the High Priest want Jesus's execution, and why did Pilate, who did not think Jesus guilty of a capital crime but who alone had the authority to order executions, agree with the High Priest's recommendation? Mark's account, which must be given priority as having been written earlier than Matthew and Luke, mentions two trials (14: 55–65 and 15: 1), though the second is very brief and could be regarded as a continuation of the main trial. His view is that Jesus was condemned by the Sanhedrin because he admitted to being the Messiah and Son of God.

In the years after the resurrection these two titles were given to Jesus by the early Christians, but that they were claimed publicly by Jesus at his trial and had the significance that they later developed, is despite his declaration in Mark (14: 62) unlikely. Until this point the synoptic gospels mention titles very little. In Mark's account of Jesus's ministry, indeed, Jesus is shown trying to stop others calling him Messiah or Son of God. What is more likely is that in the early church it seemed particularly appropriate that the claim to these titles should have had their origin at Jesus's trial.

Caiaphas and his peers had decided to arrest Jesus and condemn him to death because of his potential as a rabble-rouser. When, at the informal trial by members of the Sanhedrin, they could not find witnesses who agreed in confirming the charge of threatening to destroy the Temple, Caiaphas resorted to provoking Jesus to claim a role that could be interpreted as blasphemy. Jesus's reply, whether non-committal or not, probably the former, could then be used to condemn him. Tearing his clothes indicated extreme sorrow at such an admission and was thus effective in convincing the court of Jesus's guilt. The statement that John puts into Caiaphas's mouth that it was expedient that one man should die for the people rather than that the whole nation should perish was justified. If Jesus's followers had stirred up a riot, it would almost certainly have had to be suppressed by the Roman military garrison with consequent loss of life. Caiaphas was almost certainly not concerned with questions of theology. His one over-riding motive at this festival period was to preserve peace.

As for Pilate's decision to order Jesus's execution, this is readily explained. The gospel stories of his vacillation and the communication from his wife are probably apocryphal. The early Christians were anxious to paint the Jews rather than the Romans as their real enemies.

They had no wish to quarrel with the Roman administration and wished to prevent interference in the practice of their religion.

The Barabbas story, too, may have been similarly invented, in order to help create this hostile attitude to the Jewish authorities. It may, however, be true because there is a reference in the Mishnah[1] to a prisoner's release at the time of Passover (though there is no mention of a Roman procurator's part in this) and Josephus[2] mentions that a Roman procurator once freed a number of prisoners. But these instances have no connexion with a regular custom at the Passover feast. With some basis in fact, however, the Barabbas story, as R. E. Brown[3] has suggested, was dramatized by the evangelists to convey the truth that 'conviction of the innocent Jesus had a negative side, the choice of evil.'

Pilate, we know from Philo's *Embassy to Gaius*[4] was well known for his cruelty and executions, many without trial. The gospel account rings completely true: Caiaphas delivered Jesus to Pilate with the charge that Jesus claimed to be a king of the Jews, and thus a threat to Roman rule; he received the Jewish High Priest's firm recommendation, questioned Jesus briefly after the customary flogging designed to elicit the prisoner's confession, and when Jesus's replies to the question 'Are you the king of the Jews?' were equivocal, had him crucified without further delay. The decision would not have caused him anxiety.

Only Luke mentions a third trial, by Herod Antipas, tetrarch of Galilee (Luke 23: 6-10). It may well have taken place but, being unimportant to the outcome, it was omitted by the other three evangelists. Alternatively, Luke inserted it on his own initiative as fulfilling the scriptures (Psalm 2: 1–2) and drawing on the tradition of Herodian hostility to Jesus. In the light of Acts 4: 26–28, which Luke also wrote, this seems more probable.

NOTES
1. Pesahim 8. 6.
2. Josephus, *Antiq. Jud.* XX. 215.
3. R. E. Brown, *The Death of the Messiah* (London 1994), Vol. I, p. 820.
4. Philo, *Legatio ad Gaium*, 302.

21

The Crucifixion

That Jesus was crucified by Roman soldiers during the governorship of Pontius Pilate is the best attested event in the whole of the New Testament. The Passion narrative is recognized as historically the most reliable and most extensive section of the gospel story. On Friday 14 Nisan AD 33 Jesus was led to a killing field called Golgotha (or skull-place) outside Jerusalem and there stripped naked and nailed to a cross, the most brutal and degrading form of execution used by the Romans. A skeleton dating from first-century Palestine, which showed broken legs and heels pierced by a nail, provides non-biblical archaeological evidence that crucifixion similar to that described in the gospels was practised then, though nailing arms or wrists was not customary. These were usually tied to the crossbar. But though the fact of crucifixion is historically most reliable, the attendant circumstances described in the Passion story are less certain. Much of the gospel accounts is drawn from the Old Testament, especially Psalm 22 and Isaiah 53 (the

Suffering Servant). To what extent did chief priests and scribes, passersby, and soldiers mock him? Were two others crucified at the same time? At what hour was he crucified, nine or noon (Mark 15: 25; John 19: 14)? Were his clothes distributed among the soldiers and according to the throw of lots? What words did Jesus in fact utter on the cross? Who were present to hear him? Was there a placard indicating his crime (a claim to religio-political sovereignty)? Was his body pierced by a soldier's spear to make sure he was dead? Did a Roman centurion grasp his real identity as Son of God? These are all questions to which there is no certain answer.

The opening words of Psalm 22, 'My God, my God, why hast thou forsaken me?', are the most likely of the utterances attributed to Jesus to be genuine, for they are recorded in Jesus's own language, Aramaic (Matt. 27: 46; Mark 15: 34), and are words of despair which the early Christian communities would have preferred not to preserve, coming from one who had hitherto shown his total faith in God his father and who was soon to emerge victorious from this ordeal.

To argue that the last section of Psalm 22 (vv. 22–31) portrays a much more confident faith in God does not lessen the sense of agony and despair of the opening verse as it stands in the record. The kingdom of God, which Jesus had preached so continuously and with such authority during his ministry, now suddenly seemed remote and unattainable. That some of his friends were present to see him die and hear those words is similarly likely to be true, although the Roman legionaries would have kept them at some distance from the cross; and who more likely than his mother and her female friends, who would be far less vulnerable to arrest than his male followers, the apostles? All the gospels agree on the women's presence, though there are minor discrepancies in their names (Matt. 27: 55–56; Mark 15: 40–41; Luke 23: 49; John 19: 25–27). Only John's gospel mentions, anonymously, the nearby presence of one of the apostles, who is John himself. Such a claim and the particularly moving declaration of Jesus to his mother are intrinsically convincing. That the synoptic gospels have no record of this incident need not discredit it. We must always keep in mind that there were in the early church, even at its outset, different groups of Jesus's followers in different places who had different memories and different understandings of their master.

As for the placard put over Jesus's head, inscribed with the charge against him ('The King of the Jews'), all four evangelists describe it, but only John says that it was written in Hebrew, Latin, and Greek. That this placard is probably authentic is borne out both by the unanimity of the gospels and by the evidence from non-Christian sources[1] that the attachment of such placards to criminals was a Roman practice. That Jesus was in any sense a political threat to Rome would not have been thus advertised by the evangelists if the charge could have been suppressed. Nowhere else in the gospels except for the Magis' question in Jerusalem (Matt. 2: 2) is 'King of the Jews' used as a religious title for Jesus, which would tend to confirm that this was Pilate's reason for condemning him.

That Jesus's body was pierced by a Roman sword before being removed from the cross is found only in John. Moreover, its provenance is the Old Testament, as

John's gospel points out (19: 36–7). So its historical authenticity must be thought questionable. Indeed much of the detailed account of Jesus's death (the two thieves and the promise of paradise to one of them, the offer of vinegar by the Roman soldier, the division of Jesus's clothes, the onlookers' insults, the darkness, the rending of the Temple veil, the earthquake, Jesus's words, and the centurion's conversion) are best explained as dramatic symbolism based on the Old Testament and adapted from the oral tradition by each of the evangelists to support their own particular theological interpretation of the meaning of Jesus's death.

There is, however, enough in the gospels and the non-Christian evidence to confirm that at least some of the horrific circumstances of Jesus's crucifixion are historically true.

NOTE
1. Suetonius, *Gaius Caligula* 32. 2; *Dom.* 10. 1.

22

The Resurrection

Introduction

Jesus of Nazareth was born, lived, healed, preached, and was crucified. There is no historical doubt about his death. That he rose from the dead cannot, however, be proved historically. It is a transhistorical event, that is, having significance that transcends the historical. Indeed if his resurrection could be proved by historical methods, God would not be the sort of God that Christians believe in, one who gives us the freedom to think and act as we choose. If we were constrained to believe, our belief would have no value for us.

Yet though Jesus's resurrection is necessarily transhistorical, and there is much disagreement in our sources as to what actually happened, there is at least the possibility that in historical terms it is true. First, the euphoria of the apostles as contrasted with their initial panic and demoralization after the crucifixion, and secondly Christian history, both point to some earth-shaking happening, for which no other explanation than the Christian is at all plausible.

The empty tomb

Before considering the change of heart that affected the eleven disciples we must discuss what happened to bring about this change. At once we are faced with many discrepancies between the gospel accounts which have caused critics to doubt the truth of what is said to have happened. Can the differing accounts be harmonized? Does it matter if they are not?

In Matthew (28: 1) two women find the tomb empty, Mary Magdalene and 'the other Mary'; in Mark (16: 1), three women, Mary Magdalene, Mary the mother of James, and Salome; Luke (24: 10) also mentions three women by name, the same as Mark except that Joanna replaces Salome. In John (20: 1), Jesus appears only to Mary Magdalene, in Matthew to the women, but not to them in Mark or Luke, and Luke in the Emmaus story specifically denies that anyone in Jerusalem had yet seen Jesus. When the two disciples return from Emmaus, they are told that since they left Jerusalem Jesus had risen and appeared to Peter, but no location of this appearance is mentioned. So there are two versions of Jesus's first appearance, one to the women at the tomb, the other to Peter.

Only Matthew (28: 11–15) describes the report of the cemetery guard who confess to falling asleep on watch and the chief priests' response, which was to pay them to spread the rumour that the disciples had stolen the body during the night. This looks like a later insertion to refute this rumour. That on the basis of such fraudulent behaviour the disciples could have developed the confidence that they showed so soon after the crucifixion is enough of a refutation of this curious story. What is significant in this context is that there was never any suggestion, even among Jewish critics, that an unsuccessful search was made for Jesus's grave.

Appearances to disciples

The Emmaus episode is found only in Luke (24: 13–35), but fits plausibly into the sequence of events of that first Easter day, between the early visit to the tomb and Jesus's appearance in the evening to the disciples in Thomas's absence. The most important difference in the two accounts of this appearance (Luke 24: 36–43; John 20: 19–23) is the gift of the Spirit in John which Luke postpones to fifty days later at Pentecost.

John alone (20: 24–29) has the moving story of Thomas's confession of faith, in the disciples' company, eight days later. It is surprising that the disciples, whom Jesus had urged to go to meet him in Galilee, are still in Jerusalem; this tends to confirm the view that this was a story which was developed in the early church to convince those who doubted the evidence for the resurrection.

As to the two appearances of Jesus in Galilee, these are expressly excluded by Luke who relates Jesus's command that the disciples remain in Jerusalem until Pentecost (24: 49). The breakfast picnic on the shore of the Sea of Tiberias, when Peter is given a threefold charge by Jesus (matching the threefold denial at the trial) is found only in John (21: 1–25) though a very similar story occurs early in Luke (5: 1–11), and the two may well be reminiscences of the same event. The other appearance, on a mountain in Galilee, described by Matthew (28: 16–20), has the peculiarity that Jesus repeats his missionary charge which he had already given in Jerusalem some time earlier (Luke 24: 49).

120

Can the stories be harmonized?

These are only some of the discrepancies but are enough to show that precise harmonization of the gospel accounts is impossible.

There are, however, two general points worth consideration. First, before we conclude that this discredits the resurrection, it is our common experience that, however careful spectators of any unusual or remarkable event may be, however recent their experience of what happened, and however accurate they believe their own account to be, it is most unusual for there not to be several discrepancies, often major ones, in their testimonies. Each of us reacts differently to the same circumstances, and each of us will have observed them from a different viewpoint.

Secondly, in the reports of such an extraordinary event as the resurrection, what is surprising is not that there are so many discrepancies, but that there are so few. From the depth of despair and demoralization, the disciples had suddenly been transformed. While no doubt they were at first frightened and unsure of what had happened, they regained their confidence and courage with remarkable speed, and had soon accepted Jesus's call to mission. It is indeed impossible to exaggerate the extent of the alteration in their outlook and behaviour. At the cross they had been terrified and had kept their distance from the three crucifixes and the Roman soldiers. The world had then come to an end for them. Their beloved leader was no more. Yet within a few days they had more than recovered their spirits. It would have been strange if in their euphoria and relief their remembrance of the extraordinary events had been uniform, let alone identical. Not only did the participants include the Eleven; there were several loyal women also, and there were other disciples such as Cleopas. Each and all would have had overlapping but different memories to pass on to their communities in the early church, in and for which the four evangelists later developed their gospels.

The main aspects
Moreover, when one considers their finished product, what is convincing is that, while there are discrepancies, the main aspects of those turbulent weeks emerge with some clarity and coherence. All four gospels, as R. E. Brown observed,[1] have a similar pattern: the apostles are bereft of Jesus, he appears to them and greets them, they recognize him, and he issues a missionary charge.

The tomb in the garden, where Jesus's body had been laid on the Friday, had no body in it on the Sunday. The early visit to the tomb by the women (for whatever purpose) is entirely what you would expect. It is the only Easter story to be found in all four gospels. It is most unlikely that only one woman went on that dawn expedition. There were probably at least two, but Mary Magdalene may well have been the only one of them to have had the vision that she is credited with. What is so striking in all the appearances of Jesus (except for that described by Paul) is that he appears only to those who have faith in him. His identity remains unrecognized until the observer believes in whom he is seeing. Sight then becomes insight.

Secondly, it was wholly to be expected that the women's report of the empty tomb should have been greeted with disbelief, and that Peter, the ever impetuous and perceptive disciple, should have rushed off to see for himself, and thus was one of the first to believe. Although there are scholars who doubt whether John in fact accompanied him (as only John's gospel suggests, 20: 3–10), it would seem strange that Jesus's special friend should not have gone too; and if, as John describes, he was the first to understand the significance of what had happened, his was not the sort of thrusting personality to wish to claim priority over Peter.

Thirdly, Jesus, either in Jerusalem or in Galilee, possibly both, issued his missionary charge, although almost certainly not in the rather formal language of the Marcan addendum: 'Go into all the world and preach the gospel to the whole nation' (Mark 16: 15–18), nor in the words given by Matthew (28: 19–20): 'Go therefore and make disciples of all nations, baptizing them in the name of the Father and of the Son and of the Holy Spirit, teaching them to observe all that I have commanded you, and lo, I am with you always, to the close of the age.' These expressions are undoubtedly developments of the early Christian communities.

Fourthly, what actually happened at the resurrection, what precise form Jesus took, was clearly beyond the descriptive power of any of those early observers. They do their best to give some account of their experience, but it is altogether inadequate. Jesus materialized in a room when the doors were locked; he seemed to Mary Magdalene like a human being, a gardener; he walked and talked like a human being with the disciples on the road to Emmaus; he ate food in the disciples' company. From time to time he disappeared quite suddenly, without warning. His body was not fully corporeal; but at the same time not ghostly. The impossibility of adequate description was only to be expected of such a unique, unrepeatable and unrepeated, event. What Paul and the evangelists try to describe are the experiences of the first disciples which made them, against every human expectation, believe that Jesus was somehow somewhere still alive, despite his crucifixion.

Jesus is risen, was the resounding message that they took into the world, and for which several of them gave their lives. In W. Marxsen's words,[2] this means: today the crucified Jesus is calling us to believe.

St Paul's account

What perhaps surprises most of all is the restraint with which the earth-shaking sequence of events is described by all four evangelists, a restraint matched by the convincing Pauline account, written about twenty years after the crucifixion, much earlier than Mark's gospel, to persuade doubting members of the Christian community in Corinth (1 Cor. 15: 3–20). It has been argued that, since Paul did not mention the empty tomb, the earliest belief in the resurrection may not have included any reference to it, but he does mention Jesus's burial, and in his letter to the Romans (6: 4) he says that Christ was raised from among the dead bodies. He could moreover not have claimed that, in addition to Peter and the other apostles, James, Jesus's brother, and more than five hundred disciples saw the risen Jesus, most of whom were still alive, if this was a lie.

History of the Church

Second only to their initial experience of the risen Christ as evidence for the historical truth of Jesus's resurrection is the spread of the Christian religion down the ages and across the world. By such a small, temporarily demoralized, community the Christian message was being preached, and the Christian way of life practised, by an ever increasing number within two decades of Jesus's crucifixion. The thanksgiving meal at which bread was broken and wine poured out in remembrance of Jesus and his sacrifice was the distinctive feature from the earliest times and has remained so till today. Jesus had told his friends to do this, to eat the bread and drink the wine and, as Dom Gregory Dix has expressed it so vividly,[3] 'they have done it ever since. Was ever another command so obeyed? For century after century, spreading slowly to every continent and country and among every race on earth, this action has been done, in every conceivable human circumstance, for every conceivable human need from infancy and before it to extreme old age and after it, from the pinnacles of earthly greatness to the refuge of fugitives in the caves and dens of the earth. Men have found no better thing than this to do for kings at their crowning and for criminals going to the scaffold; for armies in triumph or for a bride and bridegroom in a little country church; ... for the wisdom of the Parliament of a mighty nation or for a sick old woman afraid to die... One could fill many pages with the reasons why men have done this, and not tell a hundredth part of them.'

This meal was the focus of the new relationship between Jesus, now the risen Christ, and his followers.

According to Matthew 28: 20 Jesus had said: 'I am with you always, to the end of time.' That his presence continued to be felt is evidenced by the remarkable spread of belief in him down the ages. From the inhuman punishment inflicted on Christians by the Roman emperors Nero and Domitian in the first century AD, through the sensibly pragmatic treatment recommended by Trajan, to the imperial recognition and approval of Constantine in the early fourth century, the Christian faith flourished ever more widely. Even after the end of the Roman empire in the fifth century, in the so-called Dark Ages (*c.* 500–1000), the Christian church preserved such vestiges of civilization as there were: law and order, education and learning. Thereafter in the later Middle Ages, Europe was Christendom. Cathedrals and churches are the built heritage of that period and later centuries, while most art – books, music, pictures, sculpture – had Christian objects or themes until the Renaissance. Even today, in an age dominated by scientific materialism, the number of believers across the world continues to increase and the power of the person of Jesus gains ever wider recognition.[4]

NOTES
1. R. E. Brown, *The Virginal Conception of Jesus and Bodily Resurrection of Jesus* (London 1979), p. 107.
2. W. Marksen, *The Resurrection of Jesus of Nazareth* (London 1968), p. 128.
3. G. Dix, O.S.B., *The Shape of the Liturgy* (London 1945), p. 744.
4. Key texts: 1 Cor. 15: 3–11; Mark 15: 42–16: 8; Matt. 27: 57–28: 20; Luke 23: 50–24: 53; Acts 1: 1–11; John 19: 38–21: 25.

23

Ascension

Part of the story of the risen Christ whose historicity is uncertain is the so-called ascension.

Luke's gospel and the same author's account in Acts differ, and the other gospels give no similar description. In Luke (24: 49–52) Jesus tells the Eleven to remain in Jerusalem until they are 'armed with the power from above' and then is parted from them. Some manuscripts add 'and was carried up into heaven'. This farewell took place in Bethany. Thereafter the disciples return to Jerusalem with joy. The implication is that Jesus left them (and ascended into heaven) on Easter day.

In Acts (1: 2–11) Jesus appears to them over a period of forty days before being lifted up into heaven in a cloud, and two men in white robes appear suddenly and tell them not to be surprised and that Jesus will return one day in the same way.

Why did Luke think it necessary to distinguish between resurrection and ascension? Has the ascension any meaning as a separate event? Jesus's resurrection showed that

127

he was alive and triumphant. Was any further experience needed to inspire faith? Can the ascension be considered historical? Is the period of forty days fact or fiction?

The last question is the least important and can readily be explained. Only Acts 1: 3 mentions this period. All other references in the gospels, Acts, and Epistles can be understood as combining the resurrection and ascension as a single phenomenon pointing to the glorification of Christ. Moreover in the history of the church there was no separate celebration of the ascension as a festival until late in the fourth century.

On the other hand, apart from the doubtfully authentic verse in Mark (16: 19), there is no narrative evidence in the New Testament contradicting forty days, and the argument of liturgical practice does not necessarily prove that the ascension was not recognized from earliest times as a separate element in the story of the risen Christ.

Furthermore the appearances of the risen Lord listed in Paul's first Letter to the Corinthians (I Cor. 15: 3–7), mentioned in the previous chapter, could hardly have all been compressed into one day. How much more reasonable that they should have spread over several weeks, called forty days to match the forty days of Jesus's temptation in the wilderness at the start of his ministry, a figure of literary convention, not historical precision. Such a period, too, would fit well the likely sequence of events immediately after the resurrection. As Professor Moule has argued,[1] the men of Galilee would have been likely to return to their home country after the week of the Passover festival and would almost certainly not have returned to Jerusalem until near Pentecost, the next major festival in the calendar fifty days later. While Luke 24: 49

seems to put Jesus's command to the disciples to stay in Jerusalem in the setting of Easter, Acts 1: 4–5 sets the same command at the season of Pentecost. His later version seems altogether more plausible.

As for the supernatural trimmings, the disappearance into overhead cloud and the sudden arrival of two men in white, these are all typical literary conventions designed to indicate the special importance of the events described. No more than us would Luke have considered that Jesus left earth like a slow rocket. He was using the historical tools at his disposal to give a vivid account of the decisive conclusion to Jesus's earthly appearances.

So, then, the ascension properly marks the climax of the resurrection story. It represents the truth of the final movement in time of Jesus from this world, with all its limitations, and the taking into heaven of the humanity which he has redeemed. As Professor Moule has expressed it,[2] 'If the eternal Word of God became incarnate at a definite time, is it not understandable that at a definite time he should also be seen to have passed on into a wider existence?'

NOTES

1. C. F. D. Moule, *Essays in New Testament Interpretation* (Cambridge 1982), pp. 57–59.
2. C. F. D. Moule, *op. cit.*, p. 63.

24

Summary of conclusions

Finally, then, we may with some confidence summarize Jesus's life and activity as follows. He was born a Jew in 5 or 4 BC in Nazareth, a village in Galilee where his father Joseph had a craftsman's business. There he spent his childhood and early adult years with his mother Mary and several brothers and sisters. In AD 29 at the age of thirty-three or thirty-four he was baptized by John the Baptist in the river Jordan and in the following three and a half years travelled continuously about the villages and small towns of Galilee. During this period he gained a remarkable reputation as teacher, preacher, and healer of the sick, and gathered round himself, as a consequence of the authority that he conveyed in word and deed, many disciples, among whom at least twelve had a specially close relationship to him. But he did not limit his company to these and shared meals and other social occasions with a wide cross-section of society, including Pharisees, tax-officers working for Rome, and others who were regarded as bad characters.

His central message, which he defined and illustrated vividly with similes and stories called parables, was that God's reign, the ideal community to which the Jews constantly looked forward, was imminent, available to those who were ready to repent. God was essentially merciful and forgiving, rather than punitive, father as well as king. Jesus saw his mission as being to all Israel, past and present, urgently requiring a positive response from all who heard it. A new ethical standard would be required; love of neighbour was all inclusive; outcasts and enemies would all be welcome.

In the spring of AD 33 (possibly 30), after a dramatic demonstration of his disapproval of Temple practices in Jerusalem, which alarmed the Jewish authorities, his whereabouts was betrayed to them by one of his closest disciples, Judas, so that they could arrest him unobtrusively at night. Earlier on the same evening at supper he had instituted a meal of thanksgiving which later became known as the eucharist. After his arrest he was closely questioned by the High Priest, supposedly found guilty of blasphemy, and handed over to the Roman prefect Pontius Pilate (who alone could inflict the death penalty) on the pretext that he was a political revolutionary who as claimant to the title King of the Jews would seriously endanger relations with Rome.

Sentenced by Pilate to crucifixion, Rome's severest penalty, he was crucified outside Jerusalem. His body, laid in a tomb after his death on a Friday, was no longer there two days later. His strong sense of mission to his fellow countrymen and the way he accepted, met, and in some form overcame, his cruel death led to his closest followers' seeing in him the long-awaited Messiah, or deliverer, of Israel, though in a redefined role as suffering servant of mankind. The cross, as representing God's supreme self-sacrifice for all, came to be seen to symbolize God's victory over evil. Soon he was worshipped by his followers as Lord and proclaimed to be God's son.

Some suggestions for further reading

Borg, M. J., *Meeting Jesus Again for the first time: the Historical Jesus and the Heart of Contemporary Faith*, San Francisco 1994.

Bultmann, R., *The History of the Synoptic Tradition*, Oxford 1968.

Burridge, R. A., *Four Gospels – One Jesus?* London 1994.

Chilton, B. D. and Evans, C. A. (eds.), *Studying the Historical Jesus*, Leiden, Brill 1994.

Crossan, J. D., *The Historical Jesus*, San Francisco, Edinburgh 1991.

Duquesne, J., *Jesus*, Berkhamsted 1996.

Edwards, David L., *The Real Jesus*, London 1992.

Evans, C. A., *Life of Jesus Research*, Leiden, New York, Köln 1996.

Evans, C. S., *The Historical Christ and the Jesus of Faith*, Oxford 1996.

Freyne, S., *Galilee, Jesus and the Gospels*, Philadelphia 1988.

Hengel, M., *Crucifixion*, London 1977. *The Cross and the Son of God*, London 1986.

Kasemann, E., 'The problem of the historical Jesus' (in *Essays on New Testament Themes*, 15–47, translated by W. J. Montague), London 1964.

Meier, J. P., *A Marginal Jew: Rethinking the Historical Jesus*, New York, Vol. 1, 1991; Vol. 2, 1994.

Meyer, B. F., *The Aims of Jesus*, London 1979. *Christus Faber: the Master-Builder and the House of God*, Pennsylvania 1992.

Riches, J. K., *A Century of New Testament Study*, Cambridge 1993.

Sanders, E. P., *The Historical Figure of Jesus*, London 1993.

Stanton, G., *Gospel Truth?* London 1995.

Theissen, G., and Mertz, A., *The Historical Jesus*, Göttingen 1996, trans. London 1998.

Vermes, G., *Jesus the Jew: a Historian's Reading of the Gospels*, London 1973. *The Religion of Jesus the Jew*, London 1993.

Witherington, Ben, *The Jesus Quest: The Third Search for the Jew of Nazareth*, Illinois 1995.

Wright, N. T., *Who was Jesus?* London 1992. *Jesus and the Victory of God*, London 1996.

Index

135

Index

ANCIENT SOURCES

142